THE SU~~~ THE UNIVERS~~~
IN BROAD SPECTRUM PSYCHOTHER~~~

Also by Wyn Bramley

THE BROAD SPECTRUM PSYCHOTHERAPIST

THE SUPERVISORY COUPLE IN BROAD SPECTRUM PSYCHOTHERAPY

Wyn Bramley

FREE ASSOCIATION BOOKS
LONDON / NEW YORK

Published in 1996 by
Free Association Books Ltd
57 Warren Street, London W1P 5PA
and 70 Washington Square South,
New York, NY 10012–1091

ISBN 1 85343 353 5 hardback

A CIP catalogue record for this book is available from the British Library.

Printing History

99 98 97 96   5   4   3   2   1

Produced for Free Association by
Chase Production Services, Chipping Norton, OX7 5QR
Printed in the EC by J. W. Arrowsmith Ltd, Bristol

This book is dedicated to the patients and supervisees who appear in it (in disguise). Without them, no worthwhile teaching would have been possible and the text would have been unbearably dull. I am deeply grateful to them.

CONTENTS

AUTHOR'S NOTE

All supervisees and patients in the text have been disguised to preserve anonymity. It should be borne in mind that many patients and many supervisees bring similar overall pictures to the supervisor and the therapist; so on occasion, where the essential clinical issue is not affected, I have combined facts from more than one 'case', again to preserve anonymity.

Fragments from a particular treatment or supervision serve to illustrate a particular teaching point being made in the text and are not meant to be understood as typical of, or a complete exploration of, that person or situation.

For the purpose of textual clarity in those instances where either gender could apply, I have given the supervisee and supervisor a feminine gender and the patient a masculine one. This conforms with my long experience in the field; that most, though far from all, therapists do happen to be female, so this apportioning of gender seemed logical. No discrimination or prejudice is intended.

1 THE SUPERVISORY AND THERAPEUTIC COUPLE COMPARED

For the purposes of this book supervision may be defined as more experienced psychotherapists helping less experienced therapists become better therapists. I like, too, the definition given to me by a trainee: 'Supervision is the bit you can't get in books, in your own life experience or your own treatment, in clinical practice or from the course. It's the goo that binds these bricks together: no goo, no wall.'

This book does not include Group Analytic, team or peer group supervision or the supervising of networks. Group Analytic supervision is written about in: *The Third Eye* (Sharpe 1994). The other sorts of supervision are discussed in: *Supervision in the Helping Professions* (Hawkins and Shohet 1991).

This volume attempts to clarify and demonstrate by means of real examples and model-building discussions, the purposes and practice of individual supervision where the supervisee – be she training still, or qualified – is doing dynamic therapy with a patient population representing a wide cross-section of society and a mixture of clinical pictures, rather than the therapist/supervisee (increasingly rare these days) who treats only pre-selected and pre-assessed patients for long-term work.

My aims are: (a) to assist the *supervisee* to come to appreciate what is reasonable and fair to expect in supervision and how, within it, she might contribute to her own learning; and (b) to help her develop the art of self-supervision (chapters 4 and 5), moving steadily toward the time when she too will want or be required to supervise, to assist the *supervisor* do a better job. Too many simply copy their old supervisors who may have operated in a professional, political and cultural climate very different from today's, producing disappointment in the supervisee, who, finding very little to read on giving or using supervision, becomes reluctant to do any herself when the time comes.

One of my unashamed motives in writing this book is to encourage all therapists, from the beginning trainee to the qualified practitioner with some years experience, to consider supervision as an integral part of their career development, a way to further their professional growth while handing on their valuable knowledge and experience to the next generation. It is important that all therapists realise from the very start of their training that supervision is no longer a sheep and goats affair, geniuses only being eligible, the work itself shrouded in mystique as if it bore no relation to the clinical activities in which therapists are engaged all the time, and from which it should be seen as a natural progression.

Any qualified therapist with some years experience should be considering doing supervision. She may not be famous, nor an academic or trainer; she may never have written a book. Her training though thorough may have been distinctly unconventional. (When I was first a Student Counsellor back in the early 1970s, we were called welfare officers and had to change our title and provide our own training by recruiting our own teachers as well as teaching among ourselves. We found and funded our own treatment and organised our own accreditation and supervision. Some of these colleagues, with whom I helped to found the national Association for Student Counselling, are now at the very top of the professional tree.) Doing supervision does not require a vastly superior intellect, nor that the practitioner has read everything ever written on psychotherapy. What *is* essential is competence in and commitment to the work, along with an ability to communicate what has been learned while doing it. It is important though, to choose a supervisee of an appropriate level of experience, just as the supervisee is advised to choose carefully (from that which is available) the experience level of her supervisor. I shall pursue this point in chapter 3.

In my book *The Broad Spectrum Psychotherapist* (Bramley 1996), I trace the course of psychodynamic psychotherapeutic treatments through a developmental sequence which has modified parallels in supervision, as I will show in more detail in chapter 3 under the heading 'Starting out as a Supervisor'. The supervisee too should be aware of this sequence so that she can help it along to her own advantage, where she is able; but the *responsibility* for its successful unfolding belongs with the supervisor.

This book on supervision can be read independently of its precursor but readers wanting further elaboration of concepts here taken for granted are referred to that publication. The sequence of therapy to be compared in chapter 3 with the process of supervision is summarised very briefly below.

DEVELOPMENTAL SEQUENCE IN THERAPY

First: where the patient (or supervisee) initially presents with anxiety, lack of understanding about the nature of the treatment, or overly distressing symptoms or catharsis, the therapist has to deploy techniques such as containment, management, education, crisis intervention and 'allowing herself to be used' by the patient (rather than imposing her own preferred way of proceeding), before conventional therapy can commence. These emergency tactics, designed to bring control into a situation where the patient feels he has none, are grouped together under the rubric of: 'The GP to the Mind function' (thus underlining the idea of therapists as adaptational creatures who must try to work with a broad spectrum of presenting symptomatology, as do general practitioners to the body, rather than selecting out especially 'suitable' – untroublesome! – patients for rarified treatment).

Fortunately this function is not always required, and the next phase, that of Assessment, can proceed. This involves the forging of a Therapeutic Alliance and a separating out of any transference, so that a Dynamic Formulation about the patient's problems can be made and a Contract agreed. My earlier book goes into each of these stages in some depth.

Post-Assessment therapy consists largely of working through the ramifications of the Formulation, in the past and present and in the transference where applicable, before starting to dissolve the transference and preparing for termination.

THE INTERACTIONAL RELATIONSHIP

Another important similarity between therapy and supervision, which needs to be made clear in this first scene-setting chapter, is that in both there is always an underlying, rarely spoken of, but real as opposed to fantasised, interactional or *intersubjective* (Lee and Martin 1991, chapter 14) relationship between 'giver' and 'receiver'. This interactional relationship can be stormy or peaceful, busily self-adjusting or stable and mostly fading into the background, but supervisee – and especially supervisor – ignore it at their peril.

The interactional relationship is one where (as in ordinary relationships, particularly new ones) whatever is overtly being said, explained, interpreted, listened to, questioned, debated or dropped, implicit reciprocal messages are constantly being sent, decoded and returned at different levels of consciousness at different times, so that each party shapes the other's productions and their own, verbal and otherwise, into a form that is jointly accessible, manageable, workable. *They actually train each other how to behave to one another.* Each one of the couple contributes to the building of a communicational bridge that will link them till the therapy is done.

Later on, the Therapeutic Alliance in treatment and the working alliance in supervision will stride over that bridge, a bridge which throughout their partnership each will from time to time maintain and/or repair, sometimes totally oblivious to what they are doing, at other times breaking into the therapeutic or supervision process to deliberately mend the bridge before one or the other falls off or through it.

Therapists and supervisors often find it impossible to acknowledge that such a stratum in therapy or supervision exists, let alone talk with the patient or supervisee in interactional terms ('Why do you think we're finding it hard to get on?' or 'I need you to be more this or that if I am to connect better with you') should it become necessary. Many are so besotted with transference manifestations in either setting, or are over-concerned to be academically/technically 'correct', that the reality of two human beings attempting to find a way through to each other, so that they can best make use of each other whatever the blockages, is forgotten or not valued. The patient and supervisee respectively are left feeling that all failures in communication must be their fault, or, perhaps worse, they ape their supervisor/ therapist in the hope of winning approval.

The truth is, in both therapy and supervision, that neither party is going to get very far without the covert, as well as overt, collaboration of the other. Supervision cannot be done *to* a supervisee any more than therapy can be done *to* a patient. Supervisee and supervisor, patient and therapist (no matter how inscrutable she *thinks* she is) participate whether they like it or not in an ever-developing and mutually modifying *real* relationship. Any transaction between the pair has to be understood against this context.

It is no use the patient just reciting his symptoms, or the supervisee just playing a tape of the session. This is akin to a child regurgitating tables on the one side, and on the other the parent or teacher correcting him. No learning (change) happens. The 'right answer' is simply memorised. A treatment interpretation from the therapist or piece of clinical advice from the supervisor, issued with all the efficiency and accuracy of a computer print-out, but without any sense of feeling or play between them, is a waste of everybody's time.

Yet it is amazing how often eager supervisees push clever and often accurate insights at patients far too soon, then become frustrated and impatient because the patient fails to respond. It is no use interpreting at a frightened and defended patient or giving clinical advice to an intimidated supervisee who feels alone and under scrutiny. Before the baby of insight arrives the couple need to build a sturdy cradle to put him in, from whence they can study, admire and play with him at their joint leisure.

Intrapsychic activity in both parties affects this interactional relationship, of course. A struggle within each person's mind has to be waged if they are to 'meet' their partner rather than merely surrender to, or be converted by, them. Each person in the supervisory and therapeutic pair has their relatively fixed internal world of bias, assumption, belief and value, which would be detectable in their day-to-day activities by watching how they manipulate and construe their external environment and the people in it to fit preconceived notions about how, for them at any rate, the world actually works. They make outer a mirror for the inner. (See R. Hinshelwood's (1994) summary of this process in chapter 10, 'Countertransference' in: *Clinical Klein*.)

Therefore, the supervisory and therapeutic pair will at first treat and evaluate each other in a way that is characteristic for them as individuals, based upon their unique set of 'inner objects'. It is not only the patient who engages in such activity, as is popularly supposed. All the training, analysis and self-discipline in the world cannot stop the therapist doing the treatment, the therapist as supervisee and the supervisor herself from doing it too, albeit from beneath their carapace of professionalism and with some degree of self-understanding resulting from their own therapy.

Each party in both couples then, has to find some areas of 'fit', some common ground where they are going to agree that for the purposes of their work together 'reality' lies. Unless patient, therapist and/or supervisor is very ill indeed, this necessary pull to mutual adjustment so they can 'do business' together is at least as strong as any pull from the 'inner objects' to maintain a transferential distortion about the other party.

It is this critical but mostly out-of-awareness adjustment between the pair, this searching for common ground while not jeopardising either person's internal *status quo* too much (such that treatment or supervision would be terminated, or one of the parties have a breakdown), that when operating well can be ignored, the treatment or supervision got on with; but which needs examination in the supervision or treatment session when things are going wrong.

The same cradle painstakingly built by patient and therapist, in which they will safely lay the delicate work of therapy, must also be fashioned by supervisee and supervisor, if there is to be sufficient trust to work as intimately and exposingly as this where required. Receiving observations about her unconscious communications can feel very threatening and critical to a supervisee. But this is beneficial in that it reminds her of how the patient might feel when she makes her interventions in their session. It might help her practise tact and facial expression as well as the right tone and vocabulary before telling him yet again what he is 'really' doing. Supervisor and therapist/supervisee should never forget that the mode of delivery is as important as the message sent!

As far as possible, while the session is in progress, the therapist reins-in her inevitable contributions to the interactional system that is developing beneath all the talking and listening, so that they will not intrude too much upon the patient who she wants to continue self-reflecting. But those contributions of which she remains unconscious cannot be controlled and when things are going well, should not. However, it is folly to assume that because she is not saying much, the patient has no real sense of who the therapist is and what she is like as a person. Each half of the couple is exploring the other at many different levels of consciousness all the time, gauging their words and actions and sending one another stop/go, more/less, silence/noise messages accordingly. The therapist may be blind to aspects of her own cueing that spoil things for the patient but which the alert supervisor is able to point out. (The supervisor too, has blind spots. Who supervises the supervisor?)

The supervisor must assist her supervisee to monitor the here and now, *two-way latent* communications that go on in sessions – in other words the interactional relationship – as well as the patient's monologic reflections, memories, dreams, associations and such, with which she may feel more comfortable. For the way the session develops is so dependent on interactional activity *between those two particular people* that it is useless for the supervisor to simply imagine herself in the therapist's place in the reported session and on that basis make pronouncements as to what should be done. This is a common supervisory mistake, aided and abetted by a nervously uncertain supervisee who longs for direct advice. The supervisor forgets that had she *really* been in the therapist's shoes, the same material from the patient may or may not have eventually emerged, but the route would have been completely different. The supervisory sense – or otherwise – made of it would have been different also, because it would have been discussed against the background of a different agreed reality between a new couple.

The supervisor can never really be a 'fly on the wall', however much the supervisee may desire it, because she does not have the same interactional relationship with the patient. The best she can hope for is an accurate report from the supervisee as to how that relationship is developing, to enable her to use her judgement and experience to help the supervisee to work out for herself what she must do. Supervision is not the panacea many want or believe it to be. Ultimately the therapist is alone; her supervisor cannot speak for or through her. No wonder inexperienced supervisees feel so vulnerable in the consulting room.

It should never be forgotten that the patient speaks at a pace, depth and transparency made possible as much by the place he feels he holds in the therapist's esteem as by the promptings of the pain inside him. The same is true of the supervisee having to open her work for inspection to a supervisor.

DIFFERENCES BETWEEN THE PROCESS OF THERAPY AND SUPERVISION

Therapy and supervision, though similar in many ways, are significantly different in others. For example, as everybody in the trade knows, in both therapy and supervision a transference as well as a 'real' attachment is likely to exist. The supervisor accepts transference from the supervisee and if it gives rise to problems works with it openly, but does not cultivate it in the same way that a therapist might. She keeps a watching brief at first, knowing that any transference will be confronted and perhaps checked by the demonstration of her actual, rather than imagined, personality as she goes about her supervising work of teaching, suggesting, asking questions, musing aloud. Usually the transference gradually fades, or fear and/or idealisation is transmuted into respect and professional comradeship, whereas in therapy it is studied, analysed and interpreted by the couple exhaustively.

Goodwill, trust, and a preparedness to take a few risks are just as vital for both partners in supervision, as in therapy, if the enterprise is to succeed. From the outset, before any contract is made to work together, the supervisory couple should be encouraged to ask one another all manner of things that in another setting might be deemed impertinent, such as 'What are your clinically weak/strong points?' 'What category of patient are you most/least at home with?' 'What therapeutic school are you most/least comfortable with?'

WHO IS SUPERVISION FOR?

With these central ideas in mind let us now ask: who is supervision for, and why is it deemed to be so essential?

Supervision benefits the therapy movement as a whole in that it promotes proper professional behaviour and attitudes in practitioners. Its widespread use, in an apprenticeship system allowing every therapist access to the level of help she currently needs (as opposed to the old two-tier system of the few aristocrats bowing graciously to the many plebeians scrabbling for any coin of attention which falls their way), maintains the highest possible standards, while preventing the relatively recent and increasingly ubiquitous practice of broad spectrum psychotherapy from falling into the hands of a few well-meaning but sometimes eccentric or outdated pillars of the therapeutic establishment. Many of these operate in quite a different, much more insulated culture from the day-to-day rough and tumble of GP's surgery, outpatient department or church, through whose doors a whole cross-section of society – some 'suitable' candidates for analytic work and some not – daily pass.

Many senior and traditionally-minded people, some very well-known and totally sincere in their wish to help supervisees, make excellent analysts but terrible supervisors for therapists who inhabit a completely different world. There is more, much more, to which the broad spectrum psychotherapist has to attend than psychoanalysis. She needs help with a diversity of adaptational approaches unheard of when many highly respected supervisors first trained. Let us have more supervisors representing all ranks of broad spectrum work who know from hard-won experience of what the job really consists.

Supervision benefits the supervisee, increasing her expertise, self-knowledge and that all-important ingredient, confidence. It benefits the supervisor also, who out of her experience with one supervisee can go on to supervise more advanced therapists who will in turn become supervisors.

It benefits training courses by adding another dimension to their trainee's learning, helping her to link theory to practice while getting valuable education from an experienced colleague from another, even if similar, 'stable'. Post-qualification supervision broadens the supervisee's theoretical and clinical base: no course can teach everything and every course has its ideological bias (and so it should if we are not to train Jacks of all trades).

Last but by no means least, supervision protects the patient from unwitting harm, while ensuring that the person into whose hands he has pledged his most vital possession, his Self, is getting the very best advice and support.

The next chapter looks at the five main areas which supervision ought to cover – promoting professional attitudes and behaviours; supervising patient care; encouraging the supervisee's professional development; supervising her education and giving her support.

2 THE FIVE AREAS OF SUPERVISION

It is virtually impossible to treat a patient successfully by proxy. Many conscientious therapists starting out as supervisors, along with trainees new to supervision, make the comforting mistake of thinking that 'correct' interventions handed on through the treating therapist will protect the patient from all harm and will ensure that he gains the insight required.

Interventions can only be 'correct' insofar as they make sense to the patient, and he can only make sense of them against the interactional, historical, emotional, Allied and transferential context built up between himself and his therapist. Such a context can be alluded to, reported on, in supervision, but not actually replicated there. The supervisor deals in possibilities, probabilities, options about what could be done with regard to the patient, but she was not and can never *be there*, so can never actually do or even demonstrate the therapy herself, as would a chef, say, or a hair stylist.

The supervisee may well need guidance as to which areas in the session it might be profitable to pursue. She may even want help in the framing of a specific intervention or set of interventions that is already in her head (rather than being put there by the supervisor). She may be struggling with an issue in the treatment sessions that she is certain is important for the patient, but wants advice on different techniques that might help break the deadlock and bring things into the open. But to accomplish this she needs to use the supervisor as a *resource*, not as a model to be slavishly copied.

Whatever she uses from her supervisor's store of knowledge must be *made her own*: she must absorb, digest, *learn* the knowledge being shown to her for herself; adapting, modifying, enlarging or jettisoning in the light of her own experience. It is no use passing on bits of knowledge that are the property of the supervisor as if she were passing the salt from one diner to the next.

Patients often know when their therapist has been to super-vision: they start talking with someone else's voice and spirit. Many years ago, when I was being supervised by someone I greatly admired and whose style I foolishly tried to copy, I had a patient who dreamt about the Three Bears. All he could remember about it was one bear endlessly repeating: 'Who's been sleeping in *my* bed?' It was the supervisor who made me see how the patient was sensing intrusion into our work. After a further session the patient started bringing stories about rabbits in safe warm burrows, and birds whose nests were too high for marauders. I took this as confirmatory material. I had thrown the supervisor out as in-structed by the patient. Bless him, he wanted me as I was, not as I wanted myself to be.

Enhanced understanding of the patient, acquired in supervision, must be converted into the therapist's own conceptual frame, based on her training and what she has made of it. Any new interven-tions decided on should be translated into her own phraseology with which the patient is familiar, and delivered if and when new material in the sessions requires it. Far too many supervisees try to manipulate fresh material from the patient in the next session to fit the new knowledge gleaned in supervision, instead of trusting the patient to bring up the unfinished matter again in his own time and own way. He may indeed be giving her a second chance in the next session, but he may also have moved on to something new, and it is her duty to follow, not to anxiously pursue a trail that has gone cold in order to keep her supervisor happy.

Most understanding that comes about in supervision can be banked for future use, with this or another patient. It is rarely wasted. It is important to remember that, among other things, super-vision is about the professional development of the therapist, not just the right interventions for a particular patient. This developmental process takes a working lifetime. Supervision is far more than a first-aid kit for psychologically bleeding patients and accident-prone therapists.

WHAT SHOULD A SUPERVISOR ACTUALLY DO?

I believe a good supervisor should routinely cover five areas, plus 'any other business' related to her particular job that the supervisee brings. First, the supervisor deals with current and long-term diffi-culties (involving both technique and understanding of the mat-erial) experienced by the supervisee in her clinical work. This much is generally accepted as the task of supervision, though supervisors vary enormously in how they execute that task.

Second, supervision should help shape the supervisee's professionalism, fine-tune her ethical sense and attitudes. Even where such an objective is not being consciously striven for, the supervisee cannot but be affected by the regular, intense relationship with a senior colleague, who for her is the very model of what a psychotherapist of skill and integrity ought to be.

The supervisor too, is in the best position to observe gaps in the all-round theoretical, technical and clinical learning of the supervisee and assist her in improving her therapeutic education.

The fourth area must surely be the most delicate for the supervisor to work on, that of enabling the supervisee to see and understand aspects of her own personality or mode of communicating that might interfere with good clinical practice, as well as identifying, owning and developing aspects of her personal gifts that promote healing. This supervisory task is generally referred to as 'promoting professional development'.

The fifth area of supervision concerns the giving of support.

SUPERVISING PATIENT CARE

The supervisor represents for the supervisee a bran-tub of ideas, techniques and clinical anecdotes with which she can compare her own experiences, as well as offering rescue packages and strategies for preventing or managing clinical crises. She borrows from the supervisor's longer and wider experience, discussing with her the moment-to-moment interactions in a given session, seeking guidance about how to correct mistakes, or where else in the material there may be links she has missed; she also traces with her the historical development of a well-established therapy, asking help and advice over new directions it seems to be taking.

While the supervisee dips into this bran-tub, the supervisor scans the case she has brought, so that once any pressing clinical problems have been dealt with, a fuller monitoring of the patient can be brought about. What might be the pitfalls and opportunities ahead for this therapist/supervisee? Which way is the plait of transference and Alliance currently turning, and where best, in the light of this, to put the emphasis when making, or deciding not to make, interventions? Is the Dynamic Formulation being firmed up by the way the treatment is unfolding, or does it need to be amended or reworked? Is the treatment team behind the scenes doing all it should? Is the supervisee giving the patient enough space or is she over-shaping the sessions to her own design? Is the pacing too slow or too fast for the patient? Is the therapist too confrontational or not challenging enough? Is she aware of her own transference to the patient?

When supervising clinical sessions an anticipatory approach is as important as a retrospective one. Prevention of mistakes is at least as important as putting them right after they have occurred. To accomplish this the supervisor attends not only to the problems and questions the supervisee consciously brings, but the wealth of other data she inadvertently reveals about how she operates as a therapist.

Case Example

I had a supervisee who had gone through a messy divorce with courage and determination and had now made a settled and successful life for herself and her two daughters. She had received a lot of support from a women's group and after it was all over started up a group of her own and took to reading feminist literature.

She brought a patient she was assessing to supervision and it was clear at once that the patient was in danger of becoming a 'cause'. She was a frail-looking, anxious, middle-aged woman who lacked any experience of independent living, having stayed with parents until her marriage, and never having had a job. Yet she was considering leaving her husband, about whom she endlessly complained, but on whom she clearly depended, mainly as an object of blame.

The supervisee felt the patient's life so far had been wasted and she should get a qualification, a job, and an independent existence as soon as possible. But she also knew that such a decision was for the patient, not for her. She saw her job as encouraging the patient to go in the 'right' direction.

I pointed out to the supervisee just how likely she was to identify with this woman and how careful she must be not to assume the same bravery and resilience existed in the patient that she herself had found when she was in crisis. Her job was to assess the patient's capacity to do any of the ambitious things she planned and to help her see how she saw her psychotherapist as her saviour, just as surely as she saw her husband as her persecutor. She was relying on my supervisee to provide the resolve she could never find in herself whenever push came to shove. I predicted that the therapist would become for the patient a substitute husband who could be blamed when it all went wrong.

The supervisee argued that 'not having the personal resources' was just the sort of argument that had kept women down for years. She herself had never believed she could get free, buy a flat, bring up two children on her own. Who knows what the patient was capable of, given some support? However, she grudgingly agreed to assist the patient to examine the marriage and her own part in it, before backing the decision to leave.

To her credit, despite her great desire to free this patient from her husband, the therapist was able to accept the mountain of evidence that accrued during Assessment, that though very unhappy indeed, the marital situation was the result of the patient's problems rather than their cause. Leaving home was not the solution. The supervisee thanked me for having stopped her from 'making an ass of myself'.

PROMOTING PROFESSIONAL ATTITUDES AND BEHAVIOURS

No supervisee would willingly bring the profession into disrepute or behave unethically, but it often happens all the same. In my earlier book (Bramley 1996) I cited the case of a supervisee who fell in love with her patient. Her feelings were sincere and she wanted help from me to prevent any exploitation of him or unprofessional conduct from her.

I tried to help her, both with the technical management of the patient and with an understanding of her own motives in the light of what she told me about previous men friends. She went through a long and painful period but in the end both patient and therapist benefited from her restraint and self-scrutiny.

Of course she knew that therapists don't have affairs with their patients. Everyone knows that. But rules alone are not enough to protect susceptible therapists. Without stringent supervision both patient and therapist, each of whom held the other in the highest regard, would have been badly damaged, the therapist in her professional as well as her private life.

Supervisors are advised to invite their supervisees now and then to review *all* their cases, not just the problematic ones. Supervisees need to show off their good work and receive praise, no less than the rest of us, while the review also offers the supervisor a rare glimpse into cases that the supervisee feels are going fine, but the supervisor may sense are not. My lovelorn supervisee left it very late before telling me of her feelings because of the shame of exposing them. I could have kicked myself for not having spotted the problem earlier, for this patient was one of only two that she never brought to supervision, once the Assessment was over.

Other aspects of professionalism include the writing up of notes, including a succinct Dynamic Formulation; what should and should not be included in replies to referrers or requests for information from relatives; how to handle the question of medication in the best interests of the patient but without alienating medical colleagues; how to negotiate a proper job specification, acquire essential working conditions such as privacy and quiet, or secure back-up services – medical cover, a supervisor, a receptionist; how to deal with fees where applicable, with professional duties and responsibilities regarding suicidal or hospitalised patients, or patients who leave therapy against advice.

These matters sound deceptively simple, but again and again I meet supervisees who do not know about them, or have forgotten their very first module of training in the rush to get on to the 'real stuff' of therapy.

Many supervisees have never given thought to the messages being sent by the way they dress; the decor of their consulting rooms; whether to collect the patient from the waiting room, or have him make his own way; whether to shake hands on a first meeting; whether and when to give a home phone number, or, especially when working privately, how to arrange cover for holidays and how much holiday at any one time it is reasonable to take. The competent professional does not leave these to chance, and the competent supervisor models desired attitudes and behaviour in the way she treats her supervisee over these same issues.

SUPERVISING PROFESSIONAL DEVELOPMENT

The supervisor cultivates self-knowledge in the supervisee, such that other patients yet to appear on the scene can benefit. During supervision sessions she will be alerted to many facets of the supervisee's professional functioning of which the supervisee herself is unaware, but about which she ought to know. These characteristics may be positive but as yet embryonic; being made conscious of them by her supervisor enables her to build on them. They may be detrimental to certain patients and need to be controlled or modified. Once alerted to their existence, the supervisee often takes these traits to her own therapy. The supervisor does not usually go into the causes of such traits but shows the therapist how they affect her work.

The supervisee may display prejudice, fear, awe with regard to certain sorts of patients (attitudinal transference), erroneously believing the patient merits such a response. Supervisors are usually the ones to eventually notice and comment. I had a supervisee with enormous distaste for men who had been to public school and, until the third or fourth time, I took her reports on the patient's unappealing personality to be accurate descriptions, not prejudice. Another supervisee, whose problematic husband had attended a famous public school, had undue sympathy and consideration for public-school types and found it hard to confront 'the poor damaged creatures'.

The supervisee may react oversensitively to certain remarks or behaviours in her patients, or indeed in her supervisor, that show an unanalysed part of herself that requires investigation; she needs encouragement to work on herself or return to therapy.

She may develop a stubborn transference to the supervisor of which she is unaware, but which obstructs the work in hand. The supervisor needs to tactfully interpret and discuss this with the supervisee (whilst of course watching any transference she may be experiencing herself, with regard to the supervisee).

It is not the supervisor's job to pry into the private life of her supervisee, but there is a grey area between therapy and supervision that needs to be cautiously and respectfully explored when situations like these arise.

Case Example

A male supervisee in his mid-thirties brought a 45-year-old woman for supervision. He had had three sessions with her but so far as I could see had not yet come to a Dynamic Formulation, indeed seemed so carried away by her that such mundane matters were forgotten.

She was an ex-newspaper reporter, wine importer and bankrupt hotel owner. She had taken a couple of years off to go round the world in a jeep, and had also managed to fit in two children and three husbands – two divorced and one dead in an accident. She had just had a travel book published and at the supervisee's request had brought him a photocopy of a chapter which he felt sure would reveal much about her personality to them both.

'But what is actually up with her?' I asked.

'Well, she's restless isn't she? The world is too small for her.

She has tremendous vitality. She just exudes energy. She's incredible. She could do anything she put her mind to.'

'She put her mind to killing herself recently, didn't she?'

The supervisee looked hurt. 'You're very sarky this morning, Wyn.'

I rapidly scanned my mental state. 'You are quite right. I am jealous as a woman and mad at you as a supervisor.'

This enthusiastic and attractive young man had always looked up to me, and though I knew it was mainly transference I was nonetheless rather flattered. This patient represented competition. I must watch my tongue.

From what he told me about the patient it seemed clear that most men of a certain type fell under her spell. He described her as a 'woman with balls', the sort of woman who lost none of her feminine appeal in competing successfully in a man's world, indeed seemed to gain more. He could only see advantage to her in this: she would always get what she wanted. He could not see her skills as in any way defensive and conveniently forgot that not all suicidal people go about complaining and miserable. Much of this woman's chopping and changing – of people and jobs – had to be a way of coping with some huge sadness or emptiness inside her. If her kind of life were working for her she would not be in therapy.

The supervisee looked glum. 'I know you think I'm smitten with her. I do think she's terrific as a matter of fact, but I'm a professional. I'm not about to do anything silly.'

'But perhaps you could show her your work, instead of looking at hers?' I asked, referring to her book chapter that he had asked to see.

The supervisee took the point. He had reacted to her like so many other men in her life, all of whom had initially adored her then found they simply could not cope with her driving, restless personality. In retrospect she found them all weak and disappointing, and resolved to take care of herself because no one else could. If he carried on the way he was going she would be disappointed in him too, and leave therapy.

I suspected the Dynamic Formulation would concern a desperate loneliness and longing to settle, disguised by the globe-hopping, glamorous exterior. But how and why this personality had developed the way it had was still a mystery. My supervisee had been so captivated by her material that he had not asked about her early life at all. She ran him and the sessions as she ran everything else.

By the end of Assessment the supervisee had uncovered a very early history of relationships that at first had seemed promising but then went sour. He traced with her her need to become supercompetent as a way of circumventing abandonment and certain betrayal. In doing this work together she began to see, and dare to hope, that this time someone else might not only be in charge but would also turn out to be reliable. I warned the supervisee that he would be severely tested on this. I predicted too, that whatever the explorations in post-Assessment therapy revealed, it would be this corrective relationship, this proof of reliability that would ultimately heal.

I am happy to say the supervisee turned up trumps, though it was a long treatment period, mainly due to the patient's difficulty in terminating: it was essential she end the therapy and not feel that it was the therapist's doing, thus letting her down like all the others.

Interestingly, a few weeks after this supervision session, as his work with the patient started to change for the better, my supervisee broke off a long-standing affair of his own, with an older married woman who had held him in thrall for months. (Needless to say, I overheard this 'on the grapevine', not in supervision.)

The personality of the therapist is her most important working tool: it needs to be regularly maintained, inspected, repaired, polished – and *admired*. Supervisors often forget to comment on the more positive aspects of a supervisee's personality: her talent for metaphor; her capacity to communicate hope or calm by sheer body language; her natural tact; her ability to show just the right combination of robustness and vulnerability; to radiate warmth without the cloying intrusiveness that so often goes with it; her toleration of negative attributions from patients without taking it too much to heart on the one hand, or retaliating on the other.

Most supervisees are all too aware of their faults and the limitations of their experience and training, but rarely see and take legitimate pride in their strongest points. These must be spelled out to them if they are to develop any confidence in their work.

When supervising trainees, supervisors should not forget the effects upon them of the course: long reading lists calculated to intimidate; the attempt to cover every theoretical school of therapy – a hundred years worth! – in three short years; the lecturers whose fund of knowledge dismays as much as inspires them; the pressure for perfect case-studies and erudite dissertations. It's enough to give anybody an inferiority complex. Supervision should offset some of this stress. When the clinical supervision is progressing smoothly, I sometimes enquire in a general way as to how training is progressing, to give the supervisee a chance to discharge some feelings and thoughts which she has to inhibit when she attends the course and is only too conscious of being evaluated.

SUPERVISING EDUCATION

As the supervisor comes to know the supervisee's work well, gaps in her knowledge and experience will become apparent. The supervisor from time to time may suggest further reading, workshops or courses, bearing in mind the many other domestic, professional and training duties to which the supervisee is already committed. Extra reading, conferences and such can be a burden as well as a pleasure. Overburdening a supervisee only serves to undermine the supportive function of supervision (see below).

Much of the therapist's educational need can be met in the supervision session itself, providing there are no clinical emergencies outstanding. For example, the supervisee may have just assessed a patient previously diagnosed as 'personality disorder', and part or all of a supervision session is given over to discussing this classification, the supervisor sharing some of her clinical experiences (but not wallowing in nostalgia) to illustrate the many contentious issues involved in treating such people.

Trust and intimacy built up in supervision allow the supervisee to ask all manner of questions she would never dream of raising in a conference hall for fear of seeming naive. I have had many clarifying discussions with very experienced supervisees who confessed long-term ignorance – one who had never seen an untreated manic patient and wanted to know just what they *do* when manic; several who failed to comprehend the notion of a 'borderline' personality; and I've truly lost count of the times I have been asked to explain, preferably in words of one syllable, just what *projective identification* is!

I have also enjoyed and learned from many a discussion about AIDS patients, hospice work, child therapy; all areas where I have very little experience. I have learned much from my supervisees about art therapy and the use of dance and drama. Medically-trained supervisees have often helped me out over the latest psychiatric medication, explained how it works. Non-British therapists have taught me much about other cultures.

As with psychotherapist and patient, supervisor and supervisee have much to teach and learn from one another. Supervision should not be a one-way street. On the other hand, supervisors should never hijack the session for their own learning, glorification or for a good gossip. It is often tempting to both parties to veer away from the work in hand, particularly where the patient who ought to be under discussion is especially difficult.

Both parties need to monitor the session time apportioned to different agenda items, but ultimately it is the supervisor who carries responsibility for boundary maintenance. This means that she needs to be aware of any unconscious attempt by her supervisee to avoid or defer work. Wanting to be popular, many supervisors covertly agree to 'rest periods' and a pattern of collusion sets in for the future.

This situation is quite different from, say, a joint agreement to allow the supervisee to discharge uncomfortable feelings about the patient in order to clear some space for thinking about those emotions. Too many supervisees want to be seen as 'good' by their supervisors and so deny or disguise negative reactions to a patient that are very much part of the material to be analysed.

But if feelings of disgust, boredom, fury, dismay or dread – to name but a few, need expressing before they can be properly thought about and learned from, a close and trusting relationship has to exist between the pair. This emphasises the need for secure boundaries round the session. Just because neither party is a patient, this does not exempt the supervisor from the responsibility of providing a safe, confidential, uninterrupted environment for the supervisee.

Many supervisees need help with organisational dynamics and relations with their professional team. Many otherwise excellent counselling courses fail to provide any teaching on these issues, so the supervisee is quite unprepared for the strains of institutional life. Almost always her fear is that some personal deficiency or her unpopularity might be responsible for inadequate communication, decision making, case management. Naturally, she is not going to volunteer such anxieties in a supervision session that feels as unsafe, untested, and unpredictable as the situation at work.

This raises important questions about whether it is feasible to be supervised by one's boss, or for that matter anyone within the organisation where the therapist works.

Education of this kind cannot succeed then, where there is too much intimacy or too little. Sessions with an external supervisor should be regular and of some duration if the proper distance between the couple is to be found. Supervision is an unfolding process, not an event; a relationship, not just a conversation. It is far more than emergency advice or 'a chance to discuss cases'. As with therapy, time and constant boundaries are needed so that each party can learn to speak the other's language, build a working alliance as resilient as any therapeutic one. Only then can any true education occur.

GIVING SUPPORT

Support is the provision of the basic and necessary conditions – physical, interactional, affective and cognitive – for the supervisee's optimal learning, both about herself and her patients. Without a doubt, the most supportive element in supervision is the boundary – or *frame* as therapeutic fashion now has it (Langs 1994) – within which that supervision occurs. The frame must be paid meticulous attention to at all times by the supervisor.

Physical provision includes the same quiet room each week with the phone disconnected. It is amazing how rarely this is respected, especially in big institutions. Changing of appointments, absences or lateness are scanned for unconscious determinants (which often say something about the reported session material) in the same non-punitive way that the supervisee examines her patient's boundary testing, though it is to be hoped that the supervisor will also be reasonable and flexible about necessary changes that do not come into this category.

Because of their colleague status as well as supervisee/supervisor relationship, many supervisors are anxious not to be seen as infantilising supervisees, so trust them implicitly over all matters concerning the boundary, quite afraid to use any legitimate authority over such things. This is a grave mistake. Even the most senior, gifted and analysed supervisee (even the supervisor herself) is possessed of an unconscious mind and will from time to time act out, struggle to acquire illicit gratifications in the session despite boundary constraints, or win inappropriate exemptions from 'the rules', thus making her life a lot easier or pleasanter, but not helping her to be a better therapist. If the supervisor cannot stand up to her, and worse if she colludes with her, the supervisee is not being protected from herself. This means she will imitate her supervisor and not protect her own patient.

Starting and ending on time can be a problem when both parties are busy professional people with full diaries, but this would not be accepted as an excuse for lateness or going over time when meeting a patient and so neither party can fall back on this to justify boundary-breaking activities.

Case Example

A supervisee was running a counselling service in a university single-handed. She was inundated with students self-referring, and under pressure from tutors and others to see urgent cases at once. She had no lunch-hour and was able to squeeze in an extra customer a day by running all sessions back to back, not taking the conventional ten-minute break between. There was no time to write notes, go to the lavatory, drink tea, shut her eyes or do stretching exercises – these being the least remarkable of the activities therapists necessarily get up to between sessions in order to refresh themselves for the next.

Naturally I tried to help her restore some balance to her day and we discussed how she might deal with over-anxious tutors, while acquiring some office help and perhaps a part-time counsellor.

She understood my reasoning perfectly, but each week reported the same pressure and exhaustion. In the supervision session she always tried to cram in more cases than was possible and I found myself trying to gallop through them as she didn't feel she could hold her worry over them for another week's supervision, for by then another list would have built up and she would get terribly behind.

I was very concerned by her stress level, the absurdity of the demands made on her at work, and I also knew there were problems with her children which had resulted in her often being late, always bursting with anxious apology.

Keen to help out a fellow therapist in trouble, I accepted the apologies. I knew all about the problems of child care from my own experience as a working mum. Because she had so many students on her books I tried to help her get the list down by tackling the most urgent cases, but even so found there was only a few minutes space for each one, and no possibility of the university paying for extra supervision. We worked as fast as we could and after each of her sessions I was exhausted, especially as I always took her over time, almost up to the next patient's appointment.

One day when she was particularly stressed, I was left without even a minute before my next patient, who I am afraid received very inferior attention that day. I took myself to task, saw how my sympathy for her plight and my misplaced loyalty to a colleague had resulted in me being so infected by her stress that I couldn't function properly either.

I made it plain the next time we met, that she would have to restrict the number of people brought so we could give first-class attention to at least one of her cases. I told her I had been remiss in allowing us to go over time because I was preaching time management to her but not practising it myself. I was being a rotten model for her.

This was no miraculous solution, but over time the supervisee gained control over her anxieties and her day and the work we did together improved. We both became progressively less, not more stressed, and the supervisee became able to place the responsibility for an inadequate service at the door of the university authorities and not herself. My next patient also benefited greatly from my calmer frame of mind!

I trust this vignette illustrates the kind of support to which I am referring. It is not about cosy reassurance, repeated 'there theres' or 'poor yous'. Maintaining a secure frame for the work takes constant vigilance and active maintenance: many supervisors feel that once the administrative rules have been laid down there is nothing more to do, except advise on the clinical work. But this is not so. Either party can destabilise the boundary and it is the duty of both to keep an eye on this. Ultimately however, the *responsibility* lies with the provider of the boundary i.e. the supervisor.

The practice of psychotherapy then, is a stressful, exhausting and anxiety-inducing business. Often, the supervisor becomes aware of dangerous stress levels in a supervisee and can prevent crises by helping her better balance her workload. It may be a matter of encouraging her to stand up to colleagues who are taking advantage of her inability to say no. It may mean helping her reassess the rate at which she can take on new or very difficult patients: there is no shame in saying sorry, but I can't take on another suicidal person at this point in time. It may mean insisting she take a lunch-break, or getting her to look more closely at why she gives upset patients an extra few minutes, at the expense of her own much-needed respite between patients.

Occasionally, it means forgetting the patients altogether and letting the supervisee blow off steam about an impossible work situation or colleague, or some sudden crisis in her own life, providing of course that such matters do not dominate every session. This is supervision not therapy. The purpose of any personal ventilation is to clear space for study of the supervisee's clinical work.

When a supervisee is overworked, tired, going through a house move or divorce, she often needs encouragement and reassurance that, even if under par, she is basically doing a competent job. Loss of confidence is not the sole prerogative of patients, neither is the right to command a willing ear or to have an almighty moan now and again.

Supervisees often need reminding that no therapist can be one hundred per cent on form, all the time. Guilt about letting patients down only adds to existing stress levels and serves no useful purpose.

I sometimes tell the supervisee of a time when I was very depressed but just able to split it off during the working day. Then I contracted flu. The combination made me feel as if I were dying. I could no longer hide my misery. But, having grave financial problems at the time, as I was just setting up in private practice, I simply could not afford to go sick. For a week I sat propped up in my chair with cushions and hot-water bottles because I ached all over. I had paracetamol coming out of my ears and could scarcely follow what was going on. My head refused to stop aching. I was a zombie. I shall never forget how ill and totally non-functioning I felt.

Not one patient noticed. When I was fully recovered from both complaints not one registered the improvement in my therapeutic performance! We therapists often exaggerate our shortcomings while underestimating our patients' capacity to make use of us even if we are at death's door.

One of my supervisees had laryngitis but felt quite well. She saw three patients that day and did not speak a word. All reported that their session had felt more productive than usual!

If the supervisee *is* temporarily failing, rather than just fearing she might be, she needs support to find the right professional help to get her back on course, a period of restorative leave perhaps, and/or containment and guidance from the supervisor such that she can relocate the resources that for the moment seem to have abandoned her.

What she probably needs most of all is to see her supervisor's calm acceptance that exhaustion or temporary psychological incapacity to do the job can befall us all. Psychotherapists are neither gods nor heroes. Their understanding of human problems is no protection against succumbing themselves. A supervisor can do much to combat the shame and guilt felt by supervisees in the throes of personal crisis, thus helping them return to normal all the sooner.

Now and then supervisees turn out to be in the wrong job. They may make wonderful lawyers, probation officers, actresses or teachers, but the supervisor senses that despite intelligence, much training, and genuine caring for others (however inappropriately expressed), their personality is so structured they will never make a good therapist. Continuing to supervise them implicates the supervisor in any subsequent harm done to patients, however unintentional that harm. Harm can be caused as much by what the therapist/supervisee consistently fails to see and do, as by what she does do.

Fortunately this situation is rare, but when it does occur must be confronted, however uncomfortable. Finding an excuse to withdraw without saying why only serves to encourage the supervisee to find alternative supervisors who might again pass on the buck, the supervisee meanwhile continuing to see, and possibly harm, patients.

If the supervisee is still a trainee, established consultation procedures of which she is aware should exist on her course, such that the supervisor can discuss her with her teachers and the course directorate, whose responsibility it is to make the final decision about whether she should be asked to leave the course. The supervisee should be told of consultations and given copies of any letters or reports about her. This honesty holds out some hope that if she does leave training her supervisor might be able to help her ventilate her feelings about it and assist her to consider a more appropriate career.

Alas, many newer courses have not yet laid down such procedures and so the trainee ends up feeling unsure and untrusting toward her supervisor, especially if she rightly suspects the supervisor is 'dropping hints' to the course staff but not coming clean with her. Trainee progress committees and the like can become bureaucratic and inhuman, it is true; but at least anxiety about the trainee's work comes into the open and she is enabled to give her side of the story and use appeal procedures should she feel she has been unfairly represented.

The postgraduate supervisee who makes the supervisor wonder how on earth she ever got through the selection process for training in the first place poses particularly difficult problems. If she really is unsuited to the work, this should be picked up in the first exploratory session between supervisor and supervisee before any contract between the pair has been made. (This is one reason why I rarely give an undertaking to supervise a postgraduate over the phone. I always like us to meet before I commit myself to what could turn out to be a very unpleasant situation.)

However, some personality problems only show themselves on much closer acquaintance. If they cannot be put right by supervision, if the supervisor is certain this is not just a mismatch between her and the supervisee, and that the supervisee is putting patients at risk or behaving unethically, she must advise the supervisee that she will be contacting her training body with her views. Closing ranks in misplaced loyalty to a potentially dangerous colleague, or moving her on to create havoc elsewhere, is not acceptable, no matter how unpleasant the alternative: patients come first.

3 CHOOSING A SUPERVISOR AND STARTING OUT AS A SUPERVISOR

Choosing a supervisor, like choosing a therapist or a partner, is a serious business. Recommendation is important, as is an investigation of the supervisor's reputation, interests, clinical experience and possibly publications. But the final decision is best taken after meeting the person to see if there is the likelihood of a good working alliance (mirroring the Therapeutic Alliance in psychotherapy).

Ideally, a supervisor with whom there is no other contact, social or professional, should be approached. This reduces the likelihood of boundary 'incidents'. Where such an unpolluted situation is impossible, the supervisee should in her own interest make sure that the contract is crystal clear, both parties aware of the demarcations between supervision, other working environments and social interaction.

Robert Langs (1994) makes much of this 'fixed frame of supervision'. In *Doing Supervision and Being Supervised*, chapter 4, he says:

> In delineating the ideal ground rules for supervision ... we are, in essence, speaking for human need and about human nature. Just as we need oxygen to breathe and state that requirement in absolute terms – there are no known substitutes – there are essential emotional needs in a supervisee (and supervisor) that must be met to allow for his or her optimal functioning as a therapist (and person). When these needs are met the supervisee flourishes: when they are frustrated there is damage and suffering.

Such separateness has its problems however, as most supervisees decide who they would like to supervise them on the strength of having worked with the supervisor, or having met her at conferences or been taught by her. In addition, although a recommendation can guarantee the supervisor's high standing in the therapy world, it cannot ensure the right 'chemistry' between the pair. And should the supervisee want a supervisor representing a specialised field of work – say adolescent work, sexual abuse, eating disorders, then supervisor and supervisee are likely to have crossed paths already.

Langs maintains that both parties have a natural inclination toward 'frame deviance', modifying the frame to suit their comfort and convenience but to the detriment of the work which should at all times be protected by the tough frame it is both parties' duty, and the supervisor's final responsibility, to monitor.

Langs goes on to point out that in the tripartite system constituted by patient, therapist and supervisor, the patient has a challenging time mastering the art of thinking and processing his material dynamically. The supervisor has an equally challenging job of making sense of the patient's contributions at one remove. But it is the supervisee who has the most demanding task of all:

> because she shifts from being therapist intervener and frame manager to being the student who is the recipient of the supervisor's interventions.

In other words, the patient and supervisor roles, however hard, are at least fixed. The supervisee is constantly moving between two overlapping frames, the most knowledgeable in one, the least expert in the other. Supervisors might pause now and then to recall their own experiences of supervision, how this change of environment affected them, and consider how their old supervisors might have smoothed the path for them. Many supervisors simply copy the way they were supervised, too deep in transferential reverence to their old supervisors to challenge or improve the method.

The supervisor need not be the same or even similar in temperament to the aspirant supervisee. Much can be gained by both parties from having complementary, and even contrasting temperaments, providing there is mutual respect and absence of fear between them. If supervisor and supervisee are too much alike in personality and/or clinical practice, they may have an enjoyable time together, but also risk the possibility of failing to see, or even reinforcing, one another's weak points, while shoring up rather than inspecting personality defences unhelpful to the patient.

Supervision will undoubtedly fail, though, if there is no personal affinity at all. Better for both to acknowledge this at the outset and part.

The supervisor is best chosen on the basis that both feel they will get along together and that though the supervisor is definitely more experienced and knowledgeable than the supervisee, there is not too much disparity in the levels of their ability and experience. It is important too that the supervisor will be able to firm up weak areas, for example teaching, research, writing, human resource management, as well as increase knowledge and skills in areas of special interest such as couple work, school counselling, NHS settings or whatever.

In selecting a supervisor it must be borne in mind that psychotherapy sessions always take place in and are affected by some kind of context and if the supervisor has no experience at all of that background there are bound to be problems. It should be admitted however, that having too much knowledge about a particular setting can produce its own difficulties. A supervisor too close to the setting may lose objectivity, may even share unconscious defences with the supervisee that enable both to survive the stress of that particular kind of work, but to which they are both oblivious. There is little point in the blind leading the blind.

Should supervision become too comfortable, almost a social occasion, the time may be approaching when a change of supervisor needs discussing. At the very least the frame needs mending. As with psychotherapy, too much anxiety in the help-seeker paralyses spontaneity, but too little reduces motivation to change and develop. In the patient's interest this should be avoided at all costs in supervision.

In any case, when finalising arrangements for the commencement of supervision (making the equivalent of the psychotherapy Contract) it is advisable to build in a review, after say six months, three if difficulties are already suspected. By then it will be clear to both parties how useful or not the partnership is and either can withdraw knowing they have given it a fair trial. Assessing each other sometimes takes time: people who doubted they could work together at the beginning sometimes find themselves glad they waited awhile.

Too many couples continue in supervision knowing that it is not meeting the professional requirements of either, but both are too reluctant to hurt the other's feelings by saying so, especially when it is felt that the supervisor is bound to have influence over the supervisee's career prospects, or might send unsympathetic messages along the professional grapevine. A built-in review, diaried at the outset, encourages both supervisor and supervisee to face each other honestly with how they are feeling and make constructive alternative arrangements where needed.

If all has gone well the review is a time for mutual compliments and gratitude, a firming up of the working alliance upon which the supervisor thrives no less than the supervisee.

The best supervisor is likely to be one who is just that bit farther along the road of professional and personal development than is the supervisee. Many new therapy graduates aim to acquire the most famous, prestigious, scholarly and clinically experienced supervisor in the region, but I am not sure this is wise. If, as a beginner, I wanted to learn to play tennis, the last person I would approach would be a Wimbledon champion. Conscious of my lowly status and inexperience I would never feel at ease with her, while she would be driven mad at never getting past the service stage. Both of us would play with gritted teeth, the tension experienced by both militating against my learning anything useful about the game.

While a supervisor at about the same level of professional maturity may be reassuring, the learning will be limited. A supervisor just that little bit ahead, who the supervisee admires but who does not awe her or arouse too much competitiveness or envy, is probably about right.

As the supervisee grows, she needs to move on to more sophisticated supervisors, just as her supervisor can begin to take on more experienced supervisees. This concept of learning by apprenticeship implies that very many more therapists ought to be doing supervision and that the current tendency for excessive reverence toward, or fear of, the few 'upper crust' therapists who do offer supervision is totally inappropriate.

Many capable therapists erroneously believe that to be a supervisor a therapist should possess superhuman clinical gifts as well as an encyclopaedic knowledge and a very high position in the professional hierarchy. This is not so. Most supervisees will testify that the learning they most valued was acquired by sharing in the supervisor's longer, but very ordinary experience; by being privy to the way she thought and felt and processed routine clinical material brought by the supervisee for supervision, as well as by the observations made about the supervisee's clinical strengths and weaknesses.

The best supervisors are those who have made every mistake in the book and so are in a position to spot other therapists' manholes before they fall down them.

Providing the supervisor works with less developed supervisees, there is no reason why any therapist with a thorough training howsoever gained, experience of her own supervision and therapy, and a few years clinical experience, should not begin the important work of supervision. Do we established therapists not have an obligation to help the up and coming generation of therapists to reach their professional maturity?

Trainers constantly complain that there are not nearly enough supervisors in the field, which can only mean for trainees and graduates that 'beggars can't be choosers'. Many mismatched supervision pairs will therefore continue, just so as to attain professional accreditation or meet course requirements. This is a travesty of what supervision is really about and does nothing to maintain the high standards required by the profession. False modesty ('Oh, but I am not good enough') just will not do. If a therapist is equipped to supervise, she is letting down the new generation, as well as turning away from her own professional development, by withholding her services.

STARTING OUT AS A SUPERVISOR

When a therapist takes the new step in her career of offering supervision, especially if she has not had the opportunity to attend a course (see reference section for addresses) or regularly meet up with other supervisors in her area, she is bound to feel anxious and self-doubting at first. She can take comfort from the knowledge that the supervision process is very similar to the therapeutic one (though there are significant differences too). She has not committed herself to the practice of new and foreign skills.

At the outset she needs to offer an introductory session, the purpose of which is mutual assessment, getting to know about how the other technically, ideologically and philosophically approaches the whole business of treating patients; whether they can communicate with each other; where personal and professional similarities and differences are; whether these are going to be a help or hindrance.

I think it should be clear from the start that this session has no strings attached; both are free to withdraw, continue, or take time to think it over afterwards. It is a good idea to exchange CVs before the initial meeting, or much time is wasted simply catching up on one another's background. This CV and any other documentation is the equivalent of the referral correspondence in psychotherapy itself.

The first interview with a prospective supervisee is not so different from the first meeting with a patient. The supervisor has to find a friendly but non-intrusive way to open the session. The supervisee may hide her anxiety beneath a submissiveness that prevents her asking what she really needs to know, or a confidence or even cockiness that she always uses when threatened, which may in turn threaten or alienate a new supervisor if she is too nervous to observe the latent process.

The supervisor should deploy silence in a non-persecuting way, so as to help the supervisee to express her needs freely. As with therapy patients a common language has then to be found. Any transferential overtones between the couple must be noted (but not necessarily commented on at so early a stage) for these are bound to affect the supervision process if they intensify with time rather than fade.

A working alliance parallel to, and as important as, the Therapeutic Alliance in the treatment situation should be striven for. While a Dynamic Formulation as defined in my earlier book is not appropriate, a similar evaluation does need to be made. Under the ordinary request for supervision, what else is being asked? What are this person's underlying hopes and fears with regard to supervision? What gaps in her experience and training need to be filled and would she and the new supervisor agree on this? How might she be feeling about this mutual assessment, right now? Why did she choose this particular supervisor in the first place? In other words, what is the *subtext* and *context* (Bramley 1996, chapter 5) of the supervisee's material?

Is the supervisee serious about wanting to learn or, having already completed a long and gruelling course, does she resent being supervised? If she is very anxious, what is she afraid the supervisor might see? Are there personality features that already hint at the type of problems she is likely to encounter with patients? By the end of this first session the supervisor should have a rough idea of just what this particular therapist might need help with, and how that particular area of concern might show up in the clinical work.

Making a supervision contract may not be as detailed or formal as making a treatment contract with the patient, but the principles and seriousness of purpose are the same. If there is much work to be done, for the supervisee is plainly insecure, inexperienced and frightened, it is no use settling for once a month or ad hoc supervision, just as it is pointless offering short-term work to certain kinds of patients. Appropriate time must be made available for the amount of work needed and attention given as to how it is financed.

Acquiring funding in the hard-pressed public sector quite often comprises the first topic of the supervisee's new supervision, the supervisor assisting her to educate the 'authorities' about her professionalism. Many supervisees pay for their own supervision to avoid conflict, when they would be better advised to get themselves and their necessary working conditions, which include *regular* super-vision, recognised and respected by their employing body.

As with the assessment of patients, the supervisee's back-up resources at home and work need inspection, without overly prying. If she is still in training then the support and tuition offered there needs evaluating, as well as the course's demands made on her time at home and in the training setting. This helps the supervisor appreciate how much or little she can pressurise the supervisee in her learning and where she ought to 'go easy'.

Any differences between the supervisor's and the course's ideo-logical views must be discussed honestly, just as it needs to be made clear whether and when supervisor and trainers discuss the supervisee.

Supervision is the one place, apart from personal therapy, where a trainee must feel able to voice her self-doubt and fear without dread of censure or negative evaluation. She cannot do this if her supervisor is also her boss or evaluating tutor on the course. If, knowing the dangers, both parties agree to go ahead anyway, it must be fully appreciated that the supportive function of supervi-sion will be at risk. Compensatory confidential structures will need to be made available – a trainee support group perhaps, or special support tutor who does *not* report to the training committee. Sometimes the personal therapist sees the supportive function as part of her work. Therapists do vary in this: some want close involvement with the trainee's professional development, so are happy to deal with the stresses and strains involved, while others see the therapy of a trainee as no different from anyone else's and believe any worthwhile course should have an inbuilt support sys-tem. (This is an important consideration for the trainee, when choosing a therapist.)

Personally, when working with trainees, I feel most comfortable with the halfway house model. The course has approved me to be the supervisor and expects me to turn in reports from time to time (I make it clear that the trainee will get copies), but the student knows I am not on the staff in any other capacity and therefore have a rather distant and formal relationship to the course. I am certainly uninvolved in their organisational politics and their gen-eral gossip. I find this provides the best basis for a trusting rela-tionship.

Has the supervisee had therapy, or is at least planning to start? This may seem an odd question as it is plainly wrong for a trainee (and even more wrong for a qualified therapist) to start seeing patients before she has had some treatment of her own, and her therapist feels she is ready to tackle clinical work. However, it is a sad fact of professional life that many of the newer courses sprouting everywhere to meet the demand for therapy training have so far failed to insist on this requirement, or are very loose about when and for how long and with whom therapy should be taken up. As a consequence many untreated, half-treated or inadequately treated therapists do come for supervision, not realising that it isn't supervision they need at this point in time, so much as therapy. But if the well-meaning supervisee – 'qualified' or 'unqualified' – is already in post and obliged to treat the agency's patients, regardless of the incompleteness of her training, what is the supervisor to do? Refuse her, knowing she will treat those patients with or without supervision? What I normally do, is accept the supervisee provided she can show that she has taken real steps toward commencing her own therapy with an appropriately qualified and experienced person.

Many of these therapists request supervision at a time when they are going through domestic or relationship upheavals, financial difficulty and exhaustion at work or in training. They vainly hope that supervision will somehow take care of all these problems. A supervisor is but a supervisor. She cannot be therapist, friend, colleague and surrogate family as well. So it is important that unrealistic (and unusually unconscious) demands made on supervision are discussed frankly during the first exploratory interview, before a commitment is made that will only wear out both parties and thus reduce therapeutic efficacy. Sometimes aspiring supervisees have to be told what they do not wish to hear: they are overstressed and must slow down, take things one step at a time, the first step being the acquisition of some quality therapy.

With trainees or inexperienced though qualified therapists it is crucial that a few boundaries are delineated. For example it is made clear that the supervisor will take responsibility for the *quality* of clinical supervision given, but the GP or hospital consultant will be medically and legally responsible for the patient's overall treatment and any consequences. When a patient is at risk of breakdown or suicide the supervisor will give all the help she can, but final responsibility lies with the head of the clinical team, or in private practice the GP. Supervision will involve helping the supervisee build bridges to, and more confidently consult with, such colleagues.

As with new patients, inexperienced supervisees need to have impressed upon them the necessity for regular and punctual attendance if they are to derive maximum benefit from a long unfolding process that is far more than the provision of 'handy hints' to clinicians. Spelling out what supervision actually is might feel patronising to an experienced supervisee, just as explanations of psychotherapy feel patronising to a senior patient, but new graduates often do not appreciate what it can and should offer and this can result in much unspoken conflict and false expectations between the pair.

It is important to uncover and answer any hidden as well as ordinary questions the supervisee has about this supervisor's particular way of working. The supervise may already have undergone various forms of supervision, good and bad, and has a right to know what she can expect at the hands of this new person.

A supervisee once asked me where I did my food shopping. It turned out that we both used the same Waitrose, but on different days. His former supervisor had met him in the butcher's occasionally and never acknowledged him. Although he knew the supervisor was trying to keep the boundaries uncontaminated, he had been hurt and resentful. We agreed that if we were to meet accidentally we would greet each other but not pursue a conversation.

Another new supervisee, still in training, indirectly communicated her anxiety about confidentiality to me by bringing three patients in a row who she said had been 'betrayed' by a sexual or business partner leaking sensitive information about them. Her indignation on their behalf felt rather overdetermined. Suddenly the penny dropped. I knew I had seen her face before somewhere but at first could not place where. A good while ago, before we were introduced, I had been leaving the theatre with one of the lecturers on her course, who had said good evening to her as we overtook them. It turned out that the lecturer had recently been appointed her personal tutor.

In order not to waste precious time, many supervisors structure their sessions, requiring material to be presented in a certain way or certain order. Some want notes of the therapeutic session under scrutiny and some prefer the supervisee to work from memory. (What she forgets may be as important as what she remembers!) Yet others use a combination or let the supervisee choose.

On the whole I leave the supervisee to decide what she needs to work on, but will comment if she seems not to have prepared herself for the session, or if she regularly uses the session to avoid certain areas in her work that could benefit from discussion. Some supervisees can't take advantage of this freedom in the early stages, as yet unable to prioritise their needs, and ask the supervisor to organise the time, or make out a schedule of topics relevant to them. This, I think, is fair enough, providing there is eventual weaning.

I sometimes plan a term's worth of sessions at a time with a trainee who is feeling rather overwhelmed by her training and by her patients. This ensures that every patient gets a look in and gives the supervisee plenty of time to plan ahead.

At the start of each session we have ten minutes 'emergency time', in which she can offload her feelings about her work, or ask for clinical or theoretical clarification of a point that has come up in the week with a patient or in her reading; or she may bring a technical point of which she is unsure, for example: 'The patient was so upset; is it always wrong to go over time a bit?' If she has nothing pressing I will ask her in this ten-minute slot how the course is coming along, or I might enquire as to the progress of a particularly difficult patient who is not on our agenda for today.

During the remaining 40 minutes with such a trainee, she begins by speaking from notes which I insist she makes after each session with the patient – the sequence of events, the unspoken themes, her interventions, the patient's response and how she felt about the pacing (inexperienced therapists always find this tricky). I usually ask a new supervisee if she'd like to get it all out first or would rather I chipped in with my comments as we went along.

No routine presentation should run over 15 minutes and I fully appreciate that it is impossible to get in everything during such a short time. However, it is sufficient to give me an overview of a session and I will ask the supervisee to supply any missing detail that I think might be important.

At the end of each term I build in a 'clinical review', the trainee or inexperienced supervisee bringing me a brief summary of all her patients. This is often a good time to fulfil the 'promoting professional development' function of supervision, highlighting both the common and disparate features of her handling of different personalities and problems. We can also see clearly how far she has developed as a therapist since the last clinical review at the end of last term, thus buttressing her confidence.

As holiday times approach, I might send her off with an injunction to forget that she ever heard the word *psychotherapy* and have a really relaxing break. At other times, as a result of more than one clinical review which has enabled me to focus more clearly on educational gaps, I might recommend a book or paper. But I do think it important not to overload trainees with dense literature when they are already up to the eyebrows in essays or case-studies for their course.

My experience is that over time the supervisee needs less and less an imposed structure and is happy eventually to bring along her own agenda. When such a state of relaxation is achieved though, the supervisor must be vigilant lest the pair succumb to temptation and become 'frame deviants'! I know of supervisors who produce tea and biscuits at this stage, when there were none before. I have to confess that I myself have been guilty of swapping novels with long-established supervisees and my only excuse is that I did it after and not during the session.

The supervision frame is much easier to abuse than the therapeutic one, because of the couple's colleague status. With the patient only one kind of relationship is permissible, but sharing the same professional world, supervisee and supervisor have much in common. If they like one another they become 'pally' very quickly.

It is not for me to lay down rules about the minutiae of the supervision setting provided, but both parties should be ever aware of the ease with which the frame they share can be undermined. The predictability, the constancy of the setting is more important than its content. One either has tea every week or not at all. (But what does the supervisor do when the supervisee is late – put the kettle on and waste more time? Risk the supervisee feeling punished by not making her a drink? Spend valuable time explaining why she is not going to waste same valuable time and break the frame by boiling kettles? And all this while assuring the supervisee that no punishment is intended?)

On meeting a prospective supervisee for the first time, the supervisor sometimes has to deploy one or more of the 'GP to the Mind' functions described in chapter 3 of my book: *The Broad Spectrum Psychotherapist* and referred to briefly in chapter 1 of this book. Before settling down into a series of regular meetings where both parties are clear about what is and is not to be done in them, the supervisor may have to contain a mass of work-related anxiety, even defuse a crisis by advising immediately about management of some situation at work that currently preoccupies the supervisee to the exclusion of all else, even a mutual assessment. Like therapy, supervision cannot always be tidy and sequential.

Some supervisees arrive for their first few sessions in emotional tatters but very quickly settle down, given a regular and predictable environment in which to ventilate their worries. Others have personal psychological difficulties warranting therapeutic intervention and supervision is not appropriate. The supervisor should make a clinical judgement about this, and take appropriate action, before a contract is made that commits her to an impossible task.

Many supervisees, whether or not they have had unfortunate experiences with earlier supervisors, are extremely wary of coming to a new one. As with a wary patient, the supervisor needs sometimes to 'let herself be used', allow the supervisee to study her, mentally walk round her, approach her gingerly, test her for trustworthiness and so forth. Many otherwise excellent supervisees are lost because the supervisor is frightened that she can't control the situation, her self-esteem is threatened by the evident suspicion or 'manipulations' of the scared supervisee, or she simply cannot be bothered to patiently sit out such an initial approach when other, more grateful supervisees are clamouring for her services.

Case Example

A recently qualified young therapist whom I shall call Terence, rang me for a preliminary talk about whether I would be the right supervisor for him. He explained that he had never heard of me or the two other supervisors he'd been recommended, but wanted to see us all before deciding. What would it cost him and when could we meet? Would I see him in the evening as he was very busy and had a lot of family commitments, his wife being ill at the moment?

I explained that I taught some evenings and others I kept aside to be with my family. Could he perhaps come at eight before his day's work started? He said yes, so we made an appointment. I explained that it would be a 50-minute session which we could review at the end to see if he wanted to come again. I told him the fee for my professional time, and how to find my house. I said that of course I understood his need to look for the right person.

He arrived 15 minutes late, explaining in great detail where he had taken a wrong turning and managing to make it sound as though my directions were not the best. As we had not met before and I didn't know what lay behind this, I let it ride, saying with a smile that perhaps we should get down to things straight away so as to make full use of the time we had left (thus making clear that while I wasn't going to make an issue of the lateness, neither was I going to add on time at the other end).

He then took out a notebook in which he had set out a list of questions concerning my qualifications, experience, publishing record and preferred method of approach, both in supervision and therapy. He was seizing the initiative, interviewing me as thoroughly as any keen newspaper reporter. I allowed him to continue with this, sensing the enormous anxiety beneath his efficient exterior and provoking questions. He said he wanted to make sure I wasn't a 'Jack of all trades' on the one hand, or too doctrinaire on the other.

Two minutes before the end he asked if I would give him some quick advice on a patient he had seen that day. I pointed out how little time was left to do the patient proper justice and the fact that he had not yet decided whether to make a commitment to our working together. Perhaps he could bring the patient next time, if he was thinking of coming again!

Once again, I was trying not to appear rejecting, but at the same time holding the frame firm, while he walked round it prodding and poking at it to see what it was made of and how resilient it was.

He cancelled the next session, because of 'a cold', two hours before it was due to take place. We made another time, and I made it clear that I would charge him for the missed session.

When we met he seemed sullen and withdrawn. After a sluggish start he began talking about the problems of the NHS, how tragic it was that poor patients could not afford private help and had to 'go to the wall' or make do with pills. I took this to be an unconscious reference to his having to pay me (he brought the cheque but had forgotten to sign it!) but I felt that it was too soon to confront him directly with this, as there was no working alliance yet, so he was bound to see it as an attack.

Instead I turned our conversation in the direction of boundary testing patients, invited him to imagine one of his own patients in the NHS persistently arriving late, or cancelling at the last minute. What kind of message might the patient be sending? We got into an intense discussion about this and he saw for himself that fees, like his own patient's lateness, were boundary issues of great import. A supervisee who can make his own links like that is worth cultivating.

At the end of the session, when he made this connection, I told him that while there was no denying that I needed his money to pay my mortgage, making him pay was also my way of preserving our supervision frame intact so that he could preserve his patients' likewise.

'Gosh', he said, 'I knew all that in theory. Did it, been there, worn the T-shirt, in our first term of training. But it's only now, because I have threatened the boundary myself, that I see the point.'

I felt it improper to ask about his personal life as I would with a patient using me this way, but it was perfectly legitimate to enquire about previous experience of supervision. Not surprisingly *perhaps, he had quarrelled with the two supervisors he had so far worked with. He felt they had tried to crush any independent thinking. The feeling I got was that they were infuriated or offended by his bold-to-the-point-of-cheekiness approach and set out to control rather than understand him. They could not tolerate non-receipt of the respect and admiration they believed to be their due.*

Eventually Terence settled well into supervision. When we finally said goodbye, we recapped these two original meetings and were able to laugh about them while acknowledging how much he had developed during our time together.

4 SELF-SUPERVISION

My term *self-supervision* refers to the private and preliminary digesting of a case and her handling of it, by the supervisee, after which she is ready to progress to more advanced work on that patient with her supervisor; or, feeling satisfied with the outcome of self-supervision she takes another, more problematic patient instead. Not every patient requires constant supervision, which can become intrusive rather than facilitating. Neither should supervision be used for the cultivation of laziness, letting the supervisor do the work of which the supervisee herself is perfectly capable.

Self-supervision is more encompassing than Casement's (1985) *internal supervision*, which refers to the essential but narrow function of constructively observing and criticising oneself in relation to emerging material while actually doing the work of therapy. Self-supervision as described here means *an overall self and case* examination *outside the session and from a certain distance*; literally giving a supervision session to oneself, but from the inside, where the richest data lie if only they can be accessed.

The non-self-supervising supervisee who borrows then repeats, parrot-like, her supervisor's thinking is not helping herself to become a better therapist. She is working from the outside in rather than the inside out. Casement (1985, chapter 2, p. 32) says:

> During the course of being supervised therapists need to acquire their own capacity for spontaneous reflection within the session, alongside the internal supervisor. They can thus learn to watch themselves as well as the patient, now using this island of intellectual contemplation as the mental space within which the internal supervisor can begin to operate.
>
> Towards the end of training, I believe that the process of supervision should develop into a dialogue between the external

supervisor and the internal supervisor. It is through this that therapists develop the more autonomous functioning that is expected of them upon qualifying.

I would only add that in ideal supervision the self-supervisor as defined above should be present also.

Most treatments develop predictably once the Dynamic Formulation is clear and confirmed by subsequent material. Others stubbornly refuse to yield to a Formulation, or appear to produce several, and the hunt is on to find the mother Formulation under which all the others can be subsumed. It is these difficult cases that often require protracted self-supervision followed by external supervision, followed by more 'mulling it over' by the supervisee. It is not true that supervision can or should always provide 'the answer' the first time.

If the supervisor is presented with raw material straight from the session, she too, is often unable to make much sense out of it. The supervisor may be competent, even inspired, but she is not a mind-reader. Supervisees often forget that the supervisor has never met the patient. The more the supervisee prepares for supervision, and clearly communicates what she has prepared, the more she (and hence the patient) will get out of it.

Whatever the supervisee thinks about the latest session with the patient is coloured by the complete history of that patient's treatment and her own changing emotional reactions to him, as well as all the moods and phases through which he as an individual and they as a couple have passed, all the tiny ins and outs of their ever developing 'real' and transferential relationship. The supervisor cannot keep this background constantly at the periphery of her vision, ready to haul in when required, as can the supervisee.

Besides, the supervisee, no matter how thorough, can only present a tiny fraction of what went on in the session and can only give an overview of the treatment as a whole. So what she does have time to bring needs to be condensed, thought through, felt through – in short *self-supervised* in the light of all the facts, feelings, counter-transferences and interactional cues that have gone on throughout the treatment and about which the supervisor cannot possibly know.

This means that the supervisee has an active part to play in her own supervision. She does not simply recount the facts about a particular session and await the Oracle's reply. She must show the supervisor how to supervise her by presenting not just the raw material, but her distillation of that material and her preliminary conclusions or hunches about it. (Similarly, the patient in therapy becomes adept at processing his own material before presenting it for refinement or corroboration to the therapist, thus teaching her how to treat him.)

It has to be recognised though, that the supervisee's very process of distillation might be what she needs help with. In this case the supervisor will indeed need to know the raw, unprocessed material – what was actually said and done by whom and in what order, to try to find out how the supervisee came to her erroneous, incomplete or 'wild' conclusion. The supervisee may constantly leave out one ingredient in the distillation process that frustrates her efforts to understand the patient – failure to see or accept certain types of (seductive? sadistic? contemptuous?) overtures from the patient for example, or her unconscious denial of some unspoken quarrel she is having with her patient. Once the missing ingredient is restored she can return to a purer distillation process on her own, then come back to her formal supervision session at a later date with new thoughts for the supervisory partnership to work on. Supervision is not a question and answer session, but *two people learning how to think together*.

A skilled supervisor will 'tune in' to the level of understanding reached by the supervisee and will know the right questions to ask, hypotheses to test, the little nudges and pokes – Maybe it's this? Could it be that? Where's the evidence? Where's the link? – that will help the supervisee to take the results of her self-supervision a stage further.

Both supervisor and supervisee are groping in the dark, but the supervisee brings with her a well-studied map (a detail, one session or part of a session cut from the greater map of the whole therapy *to which only she has access*); while the supervisor supplies her torch of experience and knowledge, making educated guesses about where it may be helpful to direct the light, and ever aware that the map itself might need amending.

I hold the rather unfashionable view that too much supervision can damage one's professional health. I feel that many supervisees, through exhaustion, laziness, fear of seeming arrogant or just sheer learned helplessness resulting from long trainee status, fail to process their own work and expect some outside expert to do it for them. Supervision should encourage rather than inhibit independent thinking, while protecting the patient and the profession from any adverse effects of a too imaginative and enthusiastic mind.

Looking back over their career, most senior therapists would agree that their best insights and techniques were developed during a clinical crisis where an immediate response was required – no time to call the supervisor, or she was on holiday at the time; or while they washed the dishes at home, musing associatively on their patient. Supervision can assist but not supplant this self-observation, this constant reflecting on why one is thinking/feeling about the patient the way one is; what it is in oneself (and maybe the patient's significant others) that is responding to him in this especial way. Overdependence on, or terror or idealisation of, a supervisor can stunt professional growth just at the time when the supervisee should be ready to take on more, not less, responsibility.

Most psychotherapy patients can be said to possess a monitoring self also, a robust self with sound critical faculties that can make an Alliance with the therapist, so that the area encapsulated by the Dynamic Formulation is in fact treated by two therapists, one literally having inside information that can be passed on to the other, professional, one to be worked over by both.

Good therapeutic practice encourages and develops this monitoring part of the patient. Doing therapy myself, I am always aware of how crowded the consulting room feels when it is going well. In this small but well-bounded space live both the patient's and my more or less permanent 'internal objects' – that is, those early prototypes that give us our unconscious view and opinion of new people (about whom we delude ourselves we are being objective). Then there is the patient's 'observing ego' and my internal supervisor, who I see as two benevolent ghostly figures hovering behind our respective chairs waiting to be consulted. There are our 'real' selves of course, thinking, talking and relating as well as cueing and responding to cues; and somewhere in the ether can be sensed the external supervisor of this case, as well as all my previous supervisors and trainers. Add these to all who 'supervised' and 'trained' my patient in the school of life and we have a full house before the people contributing to his current problems, and who he has come to discuss, are even mentioned.

This situation has its parallel in supervision. Before either party opens her mouth the room is humming with multiple 'voices', some of which will be conversed with, and others which on this occasion are not relevant to the job in hand and can be screened out.

Some supervisors become very stuck with a case because they see the supervision session as only a population of two, while others are so intellectually fascinated by the relationships between and among the characters in the room (a double cast, now that both the treatment session and the supervision session are under study) that the patient as a suffering human being is forgotten.

What is required in both these cases is that the supervisor engage in some internal and self-supervision of her own!

Alas, self-supervision cannot be taught by a series of instructions, any more than the patient can be 'instructed' to free associate. But in both cases the right setting and relationship will enable the supervisee and patient respectively to *gradually learn for him or herself*. In both cases what is required is a certain frame of mind, a special kind of attention, not a set of skills and exercises.

The supervisee will go a long way toward learning self-supervision by listening to a supervisor who is willing to muse aloud about the clinical material presented, as well as the *way* it is presented; who will comment on possible intrusions into the presented treatment session and/or the supervision session by invisible people present in the room; who will share her educated guesses; who will demonstrate her ability to fantasise freely about a patient's productions, to generate ideas, while making clear that she will never mistake fantasy for fact; who can sift and when necessary discard theoretical possibilities; who notes omissions as well as commissions in the patient and in the supervisee; who will pare away superfluous data, trawl for missing material, test and retest for evidence to back her hunches. Such activity is automatic for the supervisor, but watching her go about it again and again models the approach the supervisee needs to adopt when alone with her thoughts about a patient. Too many therapists waste precious energy in worrying about or feeling guilty over their patients when a bit of disciplined self-supervision would do a lot more good.

Self-supervision then is not so much taught as imbibed with 'mother's milk'. In other words supervisees should be allowed to see the supervisor at *work*; virtually talking to herself, but out loud, about the material under study. Many supervisors believe that they should model ideal therapist behaviour and so hide their mental meanderings and little journeys up blind alleys under a solemn, attentive silence that makes the anguished supervisee dig about for more material and yet more, until a polished and perfect pronouncement can be made by the 'correct' supervisor. The supervisor may well arrive at a new and valuable insight but the supervisee will have no idea how she got there so can never make the same journey herself.

Similarly, therapists must show their patients *how* to think, not just *what* to think. Patients should be enabled to continue their therapy self-reliantly after their dealings with the therapist have been terminated. Neither therapist nor supervisor should hang on to power and influence by mystification or keeping secrets. On the other hand of course, it is important not to be so open to inspection that their occasional inchoateness, their 'mad bits', muddle or frighten their partner. Selective openness, the allowing of the other party to see to a great extent how they think as well as what they think is not consciously contrived. It is something observable that the supervisor or therapist *is* (*has become, with experience and growing wisdom*), not something she *does*.

The best way to demonstrate self-supervision is by discussing an actual patient and an actual therapist (myself). For the sake of clarity I will keep the external supervisor out of the picture altogether. This is a patient with personality problems whom I found difficult to understand in the early stages, but about whom I felt much better after a long self-supervision session which I shall describe in detail in the next chapter.

To convey this confusion authentically I must first confuse the reader. If at the beginning of the next chapter you fail to find a pattern or thread in this woman's story and self-presentation, it reflects the complexity of her personality; it is not that you, dear reader, are losing your grip!

First I will make some brief comments on the so-called 'personality disorders' trusting that this will illumine why this totally sane, intelligent woman was nonetheless so puzzling to work with during the Assessment. Then I shall make a few remarks about the way I personally approach self-supervision. After that we are ready to meet the patient.

PERSONALITY DISORDERS

As stated earlier, most patients, at least embryonically, possess a watching, rational self that can be developed in therapy and used to evaluate the 'poorly' self's doings and have a caring attitude toward it. It is this self that the therapist cultivates in making the Therapeutic Alliance.

'Personality disorders' (and there are several categories of these, ill-defined and much argued over) cannot be so detached about themselves, *because it is the whole self – not just a neurotic section – that is the problem to be treated.* There is little and sometimes no uncontaminated observing self and what there is is far from consistent, though that self may feel perfectly rational and consistent to the patient. The Alliance therefore is bound to be affected and cannot be relied on to get the treatment couple through a crisis. Therapists are wise to try to deal with patients at the more extreme end of this diagnostic category only in a specially designed setting which can cope with impulsive acting out, unpredictable swings of mood, and disregard for therapeutic boundaries.

These patients are difficult to treat (some would say impossible) not least because they try to make their lives more bearable by deploying highly manipulative but subtle *behaviours* which to them seem normal and rational and which they can often eloquently justify. There is no desire to change behaviours or fixed attitudes for there is nothing wrong with them: it is the other party, including the therapist, who has got it all wrong, is not seeing straight. Yet their lives and relationships, because of their personality, may be in a great mess. They certainly feel pain, and want relief from it.

Can such personal qualities be coped with in dynamic psychotherapy? All therapists know from their training that that impulse/fantasy/desire which is *enacted* (i.e. behaviour, including mental behaviour such as the adopting of a fixed attitude) is no longer available for analysis, because *the feeling/need driving the behaviour is satisfied by the behaviour*. Put crudely, if you shout your head off, your anger goes away, and you are no longer so interested in working out where it came from. This is one of the critical reasons for having a taboo on touch in individual and group psychotherapy: the patient may feel better if he gives or is given a cuddle but he will be none the wiser about why he was no miserable in the first place, being now too comforted to care.

Most patients can appreciate and receive from their therapist the many ways of showing concern that don't have to be physical, and can stand emotional frustration long enough to share and look at it; but for the person with personality problems, not to be allowed to *enact*, discharge his feeling, is intolerable. For him resorting to a new *behaviour* (and manipulating words is as much a behaviour as hitting the therapist over the head) is an automatic reaction to psychic stress; he cannot, as the jargon has it, 'stay with it'. *Gratification of his desires and freedom from frustration matter more to him than gaining an understanding of where such desires and pain came from.* The therapist ends up feeling that the patient does not really want to change, but is seeking ever more effective ways of getting her to meet his needs and wishes while joining him in his idiosyncratic view of the world.

Such patients almost always have a bulging medical folder, the history going back years. They have usually had several therapists, clinics and doctors trying to find the right treatment, and often they have had several very specialist or experimental treatments. They may carry physical and mental scars as a result, which can produce very powerful protective reactions in a new therapist who resolves to be the one who will put it all right.

I shall present a patient I believe to have been not quite a personality *disorder*. Her relationships though problematic were not sufficiently dysfunctional, nor her manipulations sufficiently extreme, and she could tolerate some degree of self-examination. There was much genuine warmth and sensitivity to others and myself, and I found myself liking her a lot, not being nearly so wary as I normally am with such patients. But who is to say where the line should be drawn? There are degrees of personality disorder as there are degrees of psychosis and many, many shades of depression.

Neither was she suffering from a *multiple personality*, though viewing her in that light was often the only way I could make sense of her material. She was not a typical 'neurotic' patient either, preoccupied with one cluster of issues, pored over by the fascinated, if unhappy, monitoring self. All that could be said about her with any certainty was that she was an extremely wretched woman *whose central conflict for most of her life was the longing for health versus the fear of getting well*.

When assessing a patient who produces what appear to be several Dynamic Formulations, and who seems one minute to be 'with' the therapist, and the next minute (or sessions) not, then the therapist left wondering if it is she who has gone awry or the patient, might examine how constant or wavering is the patient's monitoring self (the invisible co-therapist). If the Formulation and the 'co-therapist' keep disappearing or changing (and assuming a borderline psychosis has been ruled out), there is a good chance that the Assessor is dealing with some degree of personality problem/disorder and she should proceed with much caution and a trip to her supervisor.

In the face of such a diagnosis, no experienced therapist will expect quick or dramatic results, and in many (though by no means all) cases management and/or chronic support, perhaps shared among the treatment team to avoid exhaustion, is the treatment of choice.

Many ambitious and overly confident, but inexperienced, therapists have got their fingers badly burned by trying to help patients accurately diagnosed as having a personality disorder. I am sad to say it is also true that many patients might have been helped to become well had they not suffered the handicap of an erroneous diagnosis of personality disorder, a diagnosis many clinicians react to as though the notes said: 'Black Death'.

SELF-SUPERVISING

Self-supervision cannot be achieved by reading an instruction manual, but all the same I shall try to smooth the path with some remarks about how I approach the whole business.

Broadly speaking, when I am supervising myself I am conducting a dialogue with myself concerning every aspect of the case so far. Although a contradiction in terms, I like to think of the technique as 'structured free association'. If I have no structure at all I quickly fall asleep or start dreaming of desert islands or composing my shopping list for the week. But too much structure would inhibit the wild flights of fancy that sometimes precede creative thought. So at the outset I meditate on a few particular topics (see below) to get the stream of associations flowing, after which the need for structure fades. If I get too lost in my associations or they dry up, I can always go back to the set topics.

First I bring into focus the life story of the patient *as he must have experienced it*. (This makes clear, I trust, the importance I place upon history-taking in the Assessment session or sessions. By the time they are drawing to a close, the patient having presented his material in his own way, any gaps in the history should be made up by discreet enquiries from the therapist. History missed at Assessment all too often accounts for problems in supervision.) I follow him from infancy, through school and adolescence, and all significant happenings and relationships to the present day. Each important incident or relationship is mused upon, putting myself in his shoes, but reminding myself from what I, the therapist, know of the history, about other things occurring around the same time, that may or may not have a connection.

Experimentally, I yoke one incident or relationship to another, ask questions (and often throw them out after!) such as: 'Where was dad then?' or: 'Had mum properly taken to the bottle at that time? Did he make up the loss by getting esteem-forming influences from his gran?' or: 'Was the quarrel with his teacher a coincidence or part of a bigger picture, his first real revolt? What inhibited him from revolting earlier and what made it possible for him to revolt when he did?' followed perhaps by: 'How much significance can be attached to the week he spent in hospital soon after? Wasn't that about the time his sister was born and gran died?'

What I am after here is *what it must have felt like for the patient*. When I know that, I can begin to imagine the kind of defences he might marshall against such feelings, unconscious strategies to cope with them, attachments he might be drawn to, or hell-bent on avoiding, as a result of them.

If some experimental link I make produces the sensation of a light bulb going on in my head, I scan all my material for confirmatory or excluding evidence, or resolve to keep an eye open for such evidence in future sessions.

Having taken a walk round the first structure, the *history*, I move on to the *Alliance* and have a play with that. How steady or variable is it? Is there any link between the occasions when it waxes or wanes – something I do or fail to do? Why, in terms of the patient's past, does it falter at the times it does? Is its weakness unchangeable due to the kind of *world view* he holds (Bramley 1996, chapter 10) and I should not bang my head against a brick wall, or could I work to strengthen it? It may be the first time he has come across the invitation to such a serious attachment and he's wary, or fears I am seducing him in some way. This does not mean he is incapable of making an Alliance, just that he is scared.

Next I fantasise about the *transference*, mine to him, his to me. It may take some while to come to accept my transferential feelings for him (if there are any). All therapists know the dangers of falling into the transference trap and accordingly many make the mistake of not checking for it – 'If I can't see it, it isn't there'. Often it is only the privacy of self-supervision that permits the emergence of transference feelings which the therapist has hitherto successfully warded off. Recognising what is being transferred to the patient is the first step in controlling it and separating it out from her other reactions.

And the patient? Is his transference to me constant, denied, half of a split, displaced on to someone else, parcelled out among several people; is it weak or strong, and why does it fade in and out at the times it does?

To elucidate his underlying feelings toward others and their reactions to him, and check them against his own (transference coloured?) reports, I *trial identify* (Bramley 1996, chapter 2, and Casement 1985, chapter 2) not only with the patient sitting opposite me in therapy every week, but also with the patient at critical stages in his personal development. (Are the ones I have always believed to be critical, *really* critical?) Sometimes much unexpected insight comes from identifying with his original family members at key stages in his life, or his current or past wives, his children, his employer. There is rarely time to constructively 'daydream' like this in the session itself, or even in external supervision.

I look again at any *Dynamic Formulation* I made in the early stages. Does it need sharpening? Is it only half right? How would my senior colleague Joe Bloggs go about formulating this one? Do I need to read round this kind of problem? Could I have cobbled together an inadequate Formulation to cover up my ignorance and protect my pride?

I then progress to examine honestly *my own feelings and reactions* to the patient, sorting out which are to do with the prejudices and preferences of my own make-up and can be put aside for the duration of the treatment, and which are feelings he is provoking in me that he probably stirs up or solicits in others, no matter what their personality: this is important material for analysis. Am I having trouble broaching such a delicate matter? What is the very worst that could happen if I did? (And what will happen or fail to happen if I don't?) I may then have a little rehearsal session with myself, trying out how the right intervention should sound.

If the patient is not improving it isn't always and exclusively the therapist's fault. Despite what he asserts, how *motivated* is he for change as opposed to other gratifications therapy can provide – an external listening ear, a sparring partner, a refuge, an excuse, sympathy?

What about the *pacing*? Could he benefit from exposure to more of the pain from which his defences are protecting him? Or is the current difficulty in treatment because he is already exposed to too much, but hiding what he sees as cowardice? Am I perhaps blind to his *cueing*, all those messages half- and unconsciously transmitted beneath, and possibly opposing, what he is actually saying? Am I only reading the cues I want to see and ignoring others?

Could the block be due to an unspoken tension in him – a sexual attraction (illicit), a state of rivalry or envy (mustn't bite the hand that feeds me), disappointment (but can't face yet another new therapist)? Perhaps I, not the patient, generate the tension – loathing (instead of analysing) his sexism, racism, the whine in his voice, his grovelling *mea culpa* admissions, or his overweening arrogance?

In addition to reprocessing all the facts of the case and the relationship between the pair trying to treat it, when I am supervising myself I always hear what I call *echoes*, and bring them for a while into the foreground of my attention. Again there is little or no time in the therapy session for this. Echoes are snippets of interaction – phrases muttered, body language curtailed, glowers and glances covered up (mine and the patient's) that I know in my bones to be meaningful but as yet I cannot decipher. So much else was happening at the time that these minute observations had to be put in storage.

In self-supervision I deal with these echoes (so-called because they reverberate within me long after the session is finished) the way I would ask the patient to treat elements of a dream he was reporting. I free associate round, between and among each echo, the way I invite my patient to consider what each part of, and person in, his dream reminds him of. As with the analysis of dreams (Freud 1976) many associations will dry up or seem not to be linked in any way. Much of the pair's work on the dream may have to be put away for another day, or discarded altogether. But often some issue will emerge from the dream associations that really moves the therapy on. So it is with much of self-supervision. It can be extremely profitable or a complete waste of time – too much data having already been repressed for me to rescue.

In my career as a therapist I have had one or two supervisors who conducted all their supervision sessions in this rather classical way. Invited to associate freely round the presented patient and then listening to the supervisor's association to my associations, led occasionally to remarkable insights, but more often sidetracked us into fascinating, detailed areas of psychoanalytic theory, while shedding little light on how I was to manage the next session.

I feel that in routine supervision the time-honoured method of reporting the minutiae of a recent session still reaps the best harvest for both patient and supervisee. The kind of supervision above, I would recommend only for use when supervisee and supervisor are both feeling very stuck and agree to experiment with a different approach.

Self-supervision is probably the only place where, with regard to a particular patient, the unthinkable can be thought, the imponderable pondered and the impossible response considered. I trust this summary of the way that I approach supervising myself makes it clear that self-supervision is a most private affair. As such it needs quiet and private conditions conducive to free (well, nearly free, for there must be a monitor) association. Gardening is good, as is solitary walking, cleaning out cupboards, or a siesta.

5 SELF-SUPERVISION: A CASE STUDY

Over the years I have treated several epileptic patients. Two women in particular, stand out. Each had a similar kind of, but far from identical, history. They both had the same complaints – marital disharmony, a belief that they were unemployable, unlovable, failed human beings, and a long-standing inability to take major decisions about running their social lives, homes, possible careers and relationships. Both had become increasingly religious over time. To safeguard 'Vera's' identity I have combined facts from both their histories, but my description of the way 'Vera' related to me, and the details of our work together, are authentic and undisguised.

Vera, 39, was referred for 12 private sessions (all she could afford) by her GP. The referral letter was cautious. She had seen countless NHS and charity therapists over a ten-year period. Few of them had satisfied her and none had been able to offer her a long-term contract. The patient knew there was something very wrong but could not pinpoint it. She now determined upon getting an Assessment from someone senior, even if she had to spend her savings on it, so she would at least know what the 'real' problem was.

Vera straight away recited the historical facts of her life. It was clear that she had recited them many times before and was weary of it.

She was born of what she called 'lower-middle' parents, with several siblings above and below her, one of whom still had intermittent depression, and one of whom was generally seen as 'very strange'. Her parents' marriage was unhappy (they divorced after she was grown up), their nightly quarrels sometimes ending in violence by both parties. Father sometimes took the strap to the children, but never her because she had epilepsy and it might bring on a fit.

Puberty had come early. She was physically well-developed and very interested in boys. She did more or less as she wished, staying out late, avoiding the rows at home as much as wanting a good time. She felt invincible because of the epilepsy, yet horribly ashamed when she had a seizure in public (about one every six weeks) and had to be brought home in a groggy, urine-soaked state, often minus a tooth, or having vomited.

There were problems at school. Though she was perfectly able, many teachers took against her, noting her interest in boys and distinct lack of interest in homework. Yet they were terrified that any challenge to Vera could result in a *grand mal*. She sounded both proud of this and deeply hurt. 'They should have helped me', she said.

Vera left school at the earliest opportunity and trained as a secretary. During her first job with a solicitor's firm she found herself pregnant and had a speedy abortion, about which she felt persistently guilty. Around the same time her parents' fighting was becoming unbearable, and she was undergoing another barrage of drug trials to see if the fits could be controlled. The pills made her fat, hairy or sleepy and she put her increasing depression down to them as well. Her boss was becoming suspicious about her sick leave and pestering her with questions. All she wanted was to 'throw in the towel and be looked after'.

Within four months she found herself married to the shy, protective, religious solicitor's clerk. They produced a daughter within the year and Vera was converted to Christianity. She took up part-time charity work with vigour, helping homeless youngsters who had come to London without any prospects. She was quickly granted additional responsibility.

For about five years all went well. Then she fell passionately in love with a fellow charity worker; 'completely besotted'. She fought temptation till she made herself ill, unable to eat or sleep. Finally she gave in. After a short, intensely sexual affair she broke it off and tried to resume her normal life. But she could not respond to her husband without fantasising about the other man and the guilt about this made her turn away from sex altogether.

Her daughter irritated her, though she loved her dearly. Guilt about being a bad mother as well as a bad wife plagued her. Both charity and secretarial work now bored her and she felt she was just too exhausted to work. She became apathetic, slovenly, envious of girlfriends who seemed to be on a career path from which she felt her epilepsy excluded her. (The fits as well as their aftermath of weakness were on the increase.)

This state of mind persisted for four years. She woke up one day, flung back the bedcovers, and announced loudly to herself: 'If I don't *do* something, my life is over, washed up!' and off she marched to her doctor. Her search for psychological help had begun.

And here she was, some ten years on, fits still out of control, unemployed, unhappily married to a dear, decent, devoted but totally unarousing man, her daughter attending the child guidance clinic for 'lack of confidence', and she herself not knowing what to do next. She supposed she must be a depressive as well as an epileptic and a failure.

So much for the historical facts, dutifully recounted. Over the next few sessions it was Vera's non-verbal communications that interested and confused me, for I could not piece together what they meant. Her appearance kept changing, as did the way she spoke, and the things she spoke of, sometimes within a single session.

For example, she had a voluptuous Italianate figure and large, dark eyes, with long, thick, black hair. She was not well off (her husband was still only a clerk) but she had the knack of arranging a swathe of scarlet fabric over a white blouse, and choosing Gypsy-style, or a dramatic Celtic type of jewellery, such as to make herself look like a veritable film star. The voice that went with these outfits was sultry, smoky, slow, even if she was talking about the price of potatoes. Yet there was nothing actressy about her presentation: it felt totally natural.

In our third session, after a recent fit, she slouched in weighed down with plastic bags, a tatty coat over her arm, looking fat, middle-aged and exhausted. Her hair was dragged back in a bun. Her voice was cracked, her speech careless. Could this be the same woman?

At yet other times in these early weeks, I wondered if she had been drinking (she hadn't), because she seemed in a sort of trance, weaving me long tales about a recent shopping trip, a meal in a cafe, or a walk in the woods, that turned out to have no real point, but which had held me totally spellbound till the end. Looking at the clock I could not believe the session was over. Had she hypno-tised me?

Sometimes she seemed full of energy, dressed more smartly, as if for the office. She would rail at the medical profession, the number of charlatans that were about – assuring me this was nothing to do with me, but I doubted that! She talked of getting up petitions on behalf of epileptics, visiting her MP. Then she would deflate like a balloon and begin to weep, saying she would never work again. She was a mess, had been a mess for ten years. No one could help her.

Whatever I took up from her material she would agree to work with till it became only slightly upsetting, and then she would change not only the subject, but also her mode of speech, her mood, her body posture, seemingly her whole personality, and I could positively feel the Alliance ebbing away, just as at other times I felt it returning, often at the most unexpected moment. None of this made any sense.

After five sessions, and still perplexed, I decided drastic action was required! I ran a hot scented bath, poured myself a large measure of scotch and retired to the bathroom, announcing that I was not to be disturbed.

After seeing her twice, I had gone through the years and years of Vera's medical notes which told me little that was new. I did see though, that she'd had a long career of consulting medical doctors/homeopaths for the various physical injuries she had sustained in her seizures, some of which were producing real and chronic complications. It was clear that she felt these people had let her down too. I also realised there had been more counsellors, some traditional, some very 'fringe' indeed, than I or the referring GP had ever envisaged. In my bath, I played with the idea: *For ten years Vera has seemed determined to get well, consulting all and sundry, yet equally determined to stay sick, medically and psychologically, sacking her helpers right, left and centre. Why?*

I next brooded on how the Alliance came and went, *as if I were treating a different patient.* I sat upright then, with a great splash.

From the amount of books written, and films made, about multiple personalities, one could be forgiven for thinking they grew on trees. But in 30 years of working in the psychiatric sector I have to confess I have never met one. I knew Vera did not qualify, but in that bath I also realised that she was as near as I was ever likely to get.

There was no one to hear or read my thoughts, no one to criticise or ridicule. *So,* I thought, reaching for the whisky, *let me organise the material I have so far as if I were writing up or talking about a multiple personality. No harm, given my whereabouts, in seeing where it might lead.*

Personality 1: The Good Wife

The Good Wife Vera would arrive with her shopping, telling me which relatives were visiting this weekend, and what she was going to feed them. On a therapeutically productive day this theme would develop into an exploration of her marriage and she would 'count her blessings', hating to be reminded by me of her sexual discontent. We might even reach back to the possible reasons for the marriage in the first place. She would weep a little about the abortion then change the subject (or the personality!) and I could get no further.

The Good Wife always grieved over her now 15-year-old daughter; there could be no doubt as to her genuine guilt over having emotionally neglected her. She constantly tried to make amends. She could only bear a moment or two's consideration of any possible envy that the daughter was not epileptic like herself, or resentment that leaving her husband would be a lot easier were it not for the daughter who needed her so badly.

Whenever I tried to make space for negative feelings concerning her domestic life, hinting that it was normal and usual to have inner doubts and resentments and that to wall them off could cause further problems, she would pause, as if momentarily tempted, then bring in Jesus. She would quote the Scriptures at me, then paint a cosy picture of her local community – the excellent school, the old people she visited who were so grateful, the church and all its social activities, her kind in-laws, and lastly her vulnerable, loving daughter, before denouncing the kind of woman who would wantonly destroy all that.

When I asked if Jesus wasn't into understanding and forgiveness as well as retribution she frowned, then explained that yes, He was like that to others, but not to her because she was so wicked inside. There was the abortion, the bad treatment of her daughter, the illicit love affair, the physical disgust she felt for the man who had loved her for all those years. No one could forgive that.

I suspected that a large denied part of her did not want to be forgiven; she fed on that erotic, aggressive, lively part, needed it to survive emotionally, while outwardly continuing her blameless life. It was this secret life that gave rise to the worst guilt of all; but if I tried to hint at this, she would produce another major shift in the session to make pursuing it impossible.

THE GOOD WIFE'S DYNAMIC FORMULATION: *The Good Wife longs for an erotic, independent existence but feels her epilepsy, religion, and her daughter prevent this, as does the fact that she is habituated to a life of security with her kind husband. She deals with this conflict by outwardly becoming the model wife and mother and secreting away – but never abandoning, hence her shame – the woman she really wants to be.*

The trouble with such a solution is that God sees all and knows the outer goodness is a lie. The impossibility of ever being forgiven, plus the intermittent recognition that sex in fantasy is no substitute for sex in fact (for deep down she remains unrepentant about the love affair), leads to bouts of inertia and depression.

Personality 2: The Siren

The Siren was easily identifiable, not just by the clothes, but by the way she swayed in her seat, stroked her upper arms, languorously stretched; the way she looked at me from under her lids, inviting me into a female conspiracy. She would sometimes talk about her teenage years as if she were talking about some other person, far far away, thus making it permissible to go into titillating detail.

The Siren knew exactly what she wanted of a man; a seducer with words, a poet, a musician, a soulmate. Everything her husband was not. Behind her hand, she would tell tales on him, his weakness, his bad dress sense, his rotten job. 'Aren't I just *awful?*' she would say, willing me to laugh with her.

The Siren would tell me about a man she met in the corner shop, how they got talking, how he bought her a cup of tea, how easy it would have been to seduce him; not that she would of course, but when you have no job, you have to cheer yourself up somehow, don't you? No harm in a cup of tea.

If I pursued the idea of employment, the risks and opportunities both practical and emotional that it might bring, she would toy sadly for a few moments with a dream of herself in a proper job, looked up to, respected, then suddenly turn into her third personality, that of the Invalid.

THE SIREN'S DYNAMIC FORMULATION: *The Siren is everything the Good Wife is denying. She lives in a dream world of what might have been, but any attempt to aid her to see that such a life is accessible if she chose it, is rebuffed, because she would have to give up all the secure benefits of being the Good Wife, along with everybody's approval and any possibility of her God's forgiveness.* Besides, her self-esteem after ten years of misery is so low she feels there is no likelihood, let alone guarantee, of her making a success of a job.

Personality 3: The Invalid

As I write this I find myself mispronouncing 'invalid' in my head as 'inva*li*d', which sums up the way Vera number 3 saw herself. As a child at home and school, she'd been powerful and intimidating because of the epilepsy, but she'd also been an outcast, an invalid person because of it, and because of the humiliating spectacle she felt she made of herself during and after a fit.

She felt invalid as a woman because of the abortion and what she saw as her inadequate mothering. She felt invalid as a professional because no one would employ an epileptic who would have to take at least one week in six off work. She felt invalid as a partner because she could not love a good husband, and she was certain the kind of man she dreamt of as a partner would never choose her.

But it was the epilepsy itself and the identity of *invalid* that sometimes goes with it, that first prompted me to use this title for Vera's third personality.

Vera's teachers must have left her with the impression that academic success was not for her, just as the girls at school left her feeling excluded from the world of friendship. Her parents' tendency to walk in frightened awe of her must have made her feel invalided out of the family too. As a teenager the only thing her epilepsy did not bar her from was sex, but the abortion frightened her into giving that up as well.

The medical notes revealed a long list of yet more people telling her directly or indirectly that she was an invalid, that she must be careful, avoid this and that, don't take risks. Many told her how to get on benefit and stay on it (*invalidity* benefit, of course), writing letters on her behalf to social work departments and even her MP.

The neurologist, for no reason I could uncover, persistently advised her to stay off drugs as they all had side-effects and there was no guarantee they would completely control the fits anyway. If she lived carefully and quietly, not getting too stressed, and leaning on her willing husband for support, she could live to a ripe old age. (He omitted to ask her if she would *want* such a life however, or to give her any choice about drugs.)

To be fair to the neurologist (patients like this make one feel very partisan), she herself had sometimes declined medication, for instance when she hoped a second pregnancy might mend the marriage, and on those occasions when she put on massive amounts of weight. But I have to say it sounded as though the consultant was after a quiet life, and having treated (or not treated!) Vera for most of her life must have suspected that putting her on medication would create as many problems as it solved. I agree with him, but she should still have been given the choice about whether to continue as an official invalid, or take her medication and her chance in the world.

THE INVALID'S DYNAMIC FORMULATION: *The Invalid hates but takes advantage of her handicap. It can be blamed* with total justification *for her lack of success in every quarter of her life, so she does not have to attempt the major feats that attract and yet terrify her.*

At the same time she knows other epileptics have made the hard decision to use drugs and endure side effects, and have as a result led fulfilled lives. Yet taking medication would give freedom and independence such that she would be tempted by all those desires both the Invalid and the Good Wife are trying to keep in check.

The solution to her conflict is to waver constantly, complain about the medical profession's ignorance, and finally to surrender to her neurologist's view.

Personality 4: The Go-getter

The Go-getter's behaviour *in the present* was a rehearsal for the career woman Vera would like to be. Unfortunately the reverse personality (Invalid) had so much influence over Vera that her hopes for work would quickly fade.

Her busy agendas reminded me of her early enthusiastic charity work, nipped in the bud by depression, before she had a chance to find out what she was really capable of. In our session she would start to organise all manner of protests, plan letters (and occasionally send them) to newspapers, draw up questionnaires for other epilepsy sufferers to fill in as a way of assessing NHS provision from the receiving end. But always she crumpled into the Invalid, and sometimes the Good Wife, before any of these projects could mature.

I tried to help her to see these schemes as positive, her career-woman self demanding expression, but the Good Wife dismissed them as silly play-acting when she ought to be attending to her family and church activities, while the Invalid told her she was far too sick to even consider such things.

The Go-getter wanted to take decisions and act on them. It must have been she who took the decisive step of abandoning teenage hedonism after the abortion for the safer world of marriage. Perhaps she had told herself she would make a new home and family that could make up for her ghastly original one. Vera's conversion to Christianity, undoubtedly genuine, had also held the powerful attraction of at last truly belonging to an enormous, supportive family, with a loving Father at its head. She would not, or could not, accept that this showed she was capable of seeing big decisions through.

It was the Go-getter too, who flung back the bedclothes and protested aloud at her imprisonment. It was the Go-getter who had an affair, who shook her fist at Jesus and refused to repent, who at 15 declared: 'At least my sex is mine: not all the teachers, doctors, friends in the world, nor the epilepsy itself can take that away from me.' The Go-getter had landed up in lots of trouble, but she had a rage to live that must at all costs be preserved if the threat of eventual suicide was to be averted.

THE GO-GETTER'S DYNAMIC FORMULATION: *The Go-getter's function is to prevent Vera's destruction by other personalities. She represents the hopeful, fighting part of the patient. If an Alliance is to be maintained at all, it will be largely via her. For as long as the Go-getter and the therapist can keep each personality alive, Vera can keep all her options open. The Siren may be erotically assertive but is not strong enough on her own, to stand up to the withering criticism of the Good Wife or the gloom of the Invalid. As a double act however, the Siren and Go-getter just about balance the other two.*

Ultimately, of course, all personalities would have to make peace with each other, i.e. become integrated. That would be the central task of any post-Assessment therapy.

The Go-getter, like the Siren, is neither good nor bad, the Unconscious being entirely amoral, but both personalities function as essential carriers of an *assertive force*, which if left to themselves might well create as much mayhem as Vera unconsciously fears; but if harmonised with (rather than remaining in conflict with) the *restraining force* of the Good Wife (also neither good nor bad) they could all gradually dispense with the necessity for the Invalid. Then Vera could begin to take some decisions about and control over her life.

Personality 5: Scheherazade

To get well, this personality, like the Invalid, would also have to be given up, but it was a pity. I became very fond of Scheherazade.

As in the *Tales of the Arabian Nights*, Vera's Scheherazade told hypnotic stories. The captive princess in the story thus literally kept her head, for the evil king who had taken her prisoner and ordered her execution kept putting it off, until he could hear the end of the tale (having fallen asleep during the hours and hours of its telling). For Vera, I was the bad king who, though not exactly chopping her head off, could delve into her mind and perhaps chop it about a bit. I had to be stopped, or at least slowed down.

This was much more than a mere defence mechanism, for any competent therapist spots aversive waffle within minutes. There was real skill and artistry in the way she unravelled her magic, successfully softening my attempts to introduce the personalities to one another. To make it work she had to metamorphose, *become* Scheherazade, sometimes for quarter, half a session. I went under her spell every time.

It was Scheherazade too, who decided when and which personality was to come to the session. If the Go-getter and I were becoming a little too chummy, the Invalid would appear. Then the Siren would walk in just at the point when I, too, felt like giving up, and we would have some salacious 'women's talk', which of course the Good Wife would put a stop to in the next session. When I got wise to all this, and would have none of it, Scheherazade herself would appear to Tell me a Story.

Perhaps I should have called Scheherazade 'The Stage Manager'?

SCHEHERAZADE'S DYNAMIC FORMULATION: *Scheherazade represents the solution to the conflict: I want my 'personalities' to meet each other, thrash out a lasting peace rather than continue their struggle for dominance, but I am not yet ready, too scared: I must play for time.*

THE MOTHER FORMULATION (under which all the others can be subsumed): *Vera cannot decide which fate is worse: a long struggle to get well, with no guarantees and the facing of immeasurably painful guilt; or giving in to her fate as an epileptic and at least using its advantages while enjoying a clear conscience. The solution that is no longer working for her is to go into as many therapies as possible, thus assuring herself she is really trying, so long as, for one reason or another, the therapist is no good or cannot take her on for the lengthy treatment she needs. Her failure to get well is then not her fault.*

I arose from my bath, crinkled, cold and clean, a slightly less worried therapist than the one who had stepped in. All the same I wondered if I ought to be writing novels rather than doing therapy. How much imaginative liberty had I taken with this case?

When the 12 sessions were over, very sad that I could not treat her myself, I referred Vera to a senior colleague in the NHS.

6 RECOGNISING WORK-INJURIOUS TRAITS IN SUPERVISEES

Many quality supervisees have dormant personality quirks that get in the way of good work with certain patients whose own peculiarities stimulate those quirks. I set out some examples below.

The supervisor needs to find a non-punitive way of pointing out these 'blind spots' as and when they show up in the clinical material presented, but it is not her responsibility to analyse their origins. That is a matter for the supervisee's own therapy and subsequent self-examination.

A central art in supervising is that of listening to the clinical material being reported, not just as information awaiting conversion into meaning according to this or that bit of theory, but as information being reported *second hand*, the supervisee having inevitably edited, maybe even unconsciously censored or exaggerated certain parts of it. In addition the supervisor needs to put herself in the patient's position, listening to this particular therapist's interventions, and processing them according to his customary way of viewing her. In other words she trial-identifies, so far as such a feat is possible, with both therapist and patient.

By the time the supervisor has won the trust of the supervisee, and is familiar with how her personality operates when she is working, some pretty shrewd guesses can be made about what the patient might really be thinking and feeling, as well as about the therapist's underlying, uncensored feelings toward the patient.

Very often no such currents are detectable because the hypersensitive areas of the supervisee's personality have not been touched by the patient. This can be a routine supervision session, as opposed to the rare ones in which the supervisor is less concerned about commentary on the patient's productions than making conscious an unconscious force in the supervisee that drives her to treat the patient in a preordained way.

THE IMPATIENT SUPERVISEE

Without being at all aware of it, this supervisee needs professional gratification as she needs air and water. A patient failing to respond is an affront to her professional pride, her need to feel she is a good therapist.

The Impatient Supervisee cannot wait for material to unfold in its own good time, but goes hunting for juicy titbits; tends to link material too quickly and without sufficient evidence. She makes an unconscious demand of the patient: 'Come on, shape up!' that her conscious, dedicated self would find horrifying.

She tends to find the GP to the Mind functions – management, containment, letting herself be used – rather irksome. This does not mean she cannot understand, approve of, or perform them, but the supervisor (and all too often the patient) senses the therapist's impatience to get to grips with 'the real problem'. She is not interested in preliminaries, or biding her time.

The patient may feel he is letting her down, is a bad patient. What if he felt as a child that he always let his mother down? What if his transference and the reality match: the therapist does indeed feel let down? History is repeating itself and because the therapist is oblivious to her professional narcissism she is powerless, without supervision, to rescue the situation.

Such therapists often enjoy short-term work, not caring much for the tedium of 'working through' that happens in more thorough therapy. They find it personally stressful to have to discipline themselves to slow down to the patient's pace; they hate having to *wait*.

I once had a patient for whom psychotherapy was a complete mystery. I used my educative function but it was no use. He now knew a lot of *facts* about therapy but he still could not, or would not, use them. A bee-keeper and farm worker, he only relaxed when talking about his bees. I made a few clever interventions, trying to link the social and industrious life of bees with his own, but they fell on deaf ears.

Each time I tried to draw his attention to relationships he reacted as if I had used an embarrassing obscenity in public and quickly went back to his bees. If I drew his attention to this avoidance he would start hinting at leaving. Just being able to talk had helped, he diplomatically fibbed; it was time to go.

In the end I realised that he found my consulting room, my language, my interest in the workings of the mind as strange as if he had landed on Mars. His bee-keeping talk was his way of holding on to his identity. Until I had accepted (and desisted from interpreting!) his complete mastery of the bee-keeping art; until he had imprinted *his* version of what life meant on to our shared setting, he could not begin to do business with me.

Only months later, after abandoning the traditional therapeutic position altogether and letting him establish with me who he was, as if we had met in a pub or at a bee-keepers' convention, did he start to tell me about his much missed dead second wife, grown-up children and his troubling first marriage.

The boredom of those months nearly drove me mad: I still have not quite normalised my relations with bees. But I believe now that the boredom cloaked anger, anger that he would not give me the material that would help me get him well. My professional pride was affronted. Only when I could allow myself to fail did I begin to succeed.

The Impatient Supervisee's unconscious assumption is that therapeutic failure is the patient's fault. Accordingly, the patient is discharged prematurely, marked down as 'unsuitable for treatment', or encouraged to take his own leave without any investigation as to why he is considering this.

THE OMNIPOTENT SUPERVISEE

The Omnipotent Supervisee is defending against impotence. She will never have to feel powerless, thus useless and despairing, *so long as she knows all the theory and techniques*, not excluding the use of her own feelings. She works, studies and examines her own psyche slavishly hard. There is a 'way forward' for every patient every time, if only she is well-read, well-practised, well-trained, well-analysed and well-supervised enough.

Such supervisees are often disappointed in their supervisors for not producing instant and/or neat solutions to any current clinical problems, or for admitting that they too are puzzled by the material so far. Sometimes such a supervisee will even believe the supervisor is withholding some knowledge or skill the supervisee desperately needs, on the grounds that she is not experienced or senior enough yet to receive such knowledge. The supervisee then works all the harder, to become worthy of the withheld knowledge. When this defence fails she becomes covertly but furiously angry at being made to face her own and her supervisor's impotence.

I had a supervisee once whose behaviour toward me was always impeccably polite and grateful. He suffered intermittently from irritable bowel syndrome and I always knew when he was in a denied rage with me for not giving him magic solutions because he'd have to excuse himself in, or just after the session, to use the toilet.

The Omnipotent Supervisee approaches therapeutic practice confident that if only she is a good and wise enough clinician all her patients stand an equal chance of getting well. She would never take delight in the minute progress of bee-keeper described above (supposing she stuck with him long enough to bring it about), but would rejoice at the quick response and complete cure of a patient ideally suited to analytic work. She is deeply reassured that all is right with the world, whenever therapy *works*. Whereas, to another less omnipotent therapist, such a straightforward therapy with a perfect patient might be felt as uninspiring routine.

Alas, all patients are not equal when it comes to the capacity to use therapy. Some have been so deprived and damaged on top of a genetic endowment that does not favour health, have become so isolated from their fellows, or rigid in their thinking, that any progress at all feels like a miracle, and the wise therapist is deeply grateful. The omnipotent therapist however, refuses to face facts, goes searching the literature or bangs on her supervisor's door demanding the Answer; it *has* to exist somewhere.

The Omnipotent Supervisee's unconscious assumption is that therapeutic failure (or only limited success) is the fault of her or her supervisor's training and experience. Therapeutic ideology, or inadequate knowledge of it, is blamed. She cannot face, and hence grieve over, the unfair realities of the world; she will never give up trying to right wrongs. Not surprisingly this supervisee frequently finds herself in difficulty when trying to help patients to come to terms with bereavement. Irreplaceability is not something she can accept.

THE MODEST SUPERVISEE

The Modest Supervisee tends to be over-reassuring to her patient, not challenging enough. The patient often feels obliged to protect and reassure her, *even when the reassuring of significant women is not a transference issue for him*. The therapist for her part often dismisses the patient's need to protect her as 'just transference' so she does not have to examine how her very real self-deprecation and fear of confrontation might affect the treatment's pacing and even its ultimate success.

The patient is afraid to show irritability, lose his temper, argue.

His therapist's humility and evident concern restricts rather than frees him; he experiences her as fragile.

A patient once complained to me about a short contact with a previous therapist. 'A porcelain vase she was, Ming dynasty. Didn't dare sneeze. Not a tough old boot like you.' He went hastily on to assure me that what he meant was one of those admirably indestructible hobnailed boots which fishermen in cartoons are forever hauling out of the water.

This supervisee uses her modesty to justify not working with a tricky transference, or the patient's need to have a fight. 'I'm not experienced enough yet. You (supervisor) could do it, but I can't.' She tends to make good Alliances with patients but then relies on them to see her through, rather than using them as a means to a therapeutic end.

In a supervision session, when I draw attention to some material crying out for an apposite intervention, I often hear remarks like: 'Oh, but I don't want to risk the trust he has built up in me. It might spoil the Alliance.' I have to point out that the whole point of having an Alliance in the first place is to make such risks possible, the consequences of those risks jointly bearable, or cause for joint celebration.

The modesty of the Modest Supervisee is an *inappropriate* modesty, keeping herself in the wrong or giving herself lowly status to guard against any show of independence from, envy of, or disagreement with her supervisor (and doubtless other key persons in her life). The supervisor is idealised, leaving her feeling most uncomfortable as she is all too aware that contempt often clings to the underbelly of idealisation.

The Modest Supervisee is like the soldier waving the white flag. Having already admitted defeat, no one will shoot him.

The Modest Supervisee needs her patient to love her, or at least never be angry at or critical of her, even if it means sacrificing the therapeutic progress that controlled experiments, risk-taking interventions and acting on hunches can bring. Similarly she wants the approval of her supervisor, whom she unconsciously believes will be touched by her humility and her admiration and will respond accordingly.

Such placatoriness, never questioning, never criticising, represents the solution to the dilemma: 'How can I keep the regard of someone I need (originally a parent?) but of whom I am envious and with whom I cannot afford to be rivalrous or angry lest they retaliate and I lose them?'

The Modest Supervisee's assumption is that problems and failures in therapy are *bound* to be her own fault: she is willing to take the blame so as to solicit approval and support to function better from 'seniors' who will then feel good about her for being the cause of their subsequent self-enhancement. She buries very deep any lurking suspicion that it may not always be her fault, or that the supervisor might be wrong.

THE NON-GRADUATING SUPERVISEE

This supervisee also aggrandises her teachers, trainers, supervisors, but the unconscious need to do this is based mainly on dependency, fear of growing up, rather than any dread of retaliation. (However, none of these profiles is mutually exclusive: hybrids abound.)

On passing the driving test, many drivers still feel they are learners, and qualify themselves, later on, when they have developed more expertise and confidence. The same is true, and I think desirable, for graduate therapists. But the Non-Graduating Supervisee is someone terrified of her coming-of-age in the profession. To make independent professional and clinical decisions, standing by what she says, believes and writes whatever the criticism and disagreement, is a frightening prospect for her. She sees such a stance as arrogance which is bound to be punished; that she is bound to be found out for the ill-prepared therapist she really is.

She always needs a therapist, a supervisor, a tutor at her back, to protect and defend her, and in extreme situations tell her what to do and how to bear awful professional situations – the death of a patient, paranoid threats to sue, failed treatments. Naturally, any therapist would seek support from colleagues over such worrying issues, but the Non-Graduating Supervisee has such resources permanently in place, whether she has problems or not, such is her fear of standing alone in the world.

Such therapists are reluctant to publish, never take a break from supervision, stay in therapy much longer than their peers and believe they cannot do without it. They are always on a course. Their faces are familiar on the conference and workshop circuit, as they desperately try to improve their credentials so as to insure against criticism. Like the Omnipotent Supervisee they cannot accept that no therapist can possibly know everything. Only when they have mastered it all will they feel ready to graduate. And so they remain eternal students.

As a result of their unconscious preoccupations such supervisees tend to be very informed, able, compassionate toward patient neediness and full of self-knowledge – except about their inability to permit themselves to graduate into a fully professional, less-than-perfect-like-the-rest-of-us autonomous psychotherapist. The rest of the professional community lose out on their contribution, because they still hide behind the skirts of guru supervisors, analysts or authors from whom they need to emotionally separate.

When this supervisee hits clinical problems she takes it as proof that she is not yet ready to run her own professional life (no matter that therapists with decades of experience still make mistakes, or fail to succeed with very difficult patients). It is almost a relief to tell herself she must go back to school; for it is safe there. Someone else can continue to take responsibility for her.

But in order to maintain this comforting cocoon, she must deprive herself of the healthy pride and pleasure that comes with self-awarded graduation, as well as the welcome into and invitation to make use of the pooled resources of the graduate community. Here, she could avail herself of more professional development as and when she felt the need for it, through consultative colleagueship, rather than continuing with uninterrupted parent–child dependency.

THE INSECURE SUPERVISEE

This supervisee is in a state of barely controlled panic until she feels she has 'cracked' a case. She does not need to have worked miracles, or to have understood everything, or reduced any symptomatology: all she needs is to feel she has 'got the hang' of the treatment, knows roughly what she is doing, and what direction she must take.

All therapists must learn to live with their ignorance in the consulting room; tolerate feeling as lost as the patient for a while; accept the wound to their pride inflicted by the state of not-knowing. Most painful of all to bear are their patient's looks or words of disbelief and disappointment as it dawns on him that the therapist for the moment is no wiser than he. It is this early phase of treatment that the Insecure Supervisee finds so hard.

Once the Alliance is made and a Dynamic Formulation is shaping up, the Insecure Supervisee blossoms. Serious difficulties arise though, with a patient whose very problem is a limited capacity to trust or attach, or a patient skilled at manipulating others. The supervisee becomes frightened, feels inadequate when she cannot make a pattern out of the disparate bits of material flying about her mind. Faced with a schizoid patient, a seriously obsessional or somatising person, or someone with a personality disorder, she becomes panicky where a more confident therapist might feel challenge, fascination, a chance to learn something new, if she can accept that results will almost certainly be less than ideal.

The Insecure Supervisee panics again, when faced with a patient whose unconscious view of the world is different from hers. Most patients, along with most therapists, believe in 'fair dos', 'love makes the world go round', 'all men are born equal', 'most folk mean well', without even thinking about it. This shared set of values is the embryo of the Alliance yet to be born. But some patients behave suspiciously, aggressively, competitively from the start, not in relation to any special thing the therapist says or does, but to *everything* she offers, prompted *not by a particular transference to her* but by their basic assumptions about the world (Bramley 1996 chapter 10).

For such a patient, trust and cooperation in any genuine sense is well-nigh impossible. Therapeutic progress is the reverse of usual: when he is ready to make the Alliance and the Dynamic Formulation has been understood by him, he is better, maybe ready to leave. The treatment tends to be long, frustrating, puzzling. Only toward the end does the therapist see glimmerings of light. The Insecure Supervisee cannot bear to be out of control for that long.

The Insecure Supervisee cannot relax into her work until she feels she is on top of things. Neither can she abide being hated, envied, scorned or rejected unless the transference producing such distortion is so crystal clear that only a mad therapist would take it personally. She can take negative attributions, so long as they make sense to her. What she cannot bear is uncertainty, any negative feelings from the patient that might have a basis in reality, or any slowness in the treatment that could testify to professional inadequacy.

The Insecure Supervisee experiences herself not as a therapeutic *instrument* for the patient's use, but as a *personality*, one that desperately needs positive feedback – i.e. the patient improving, or at the very least her knowing what might be going on. She has not yet learned to put her need for self-approval, for 'results' on one side, and to view the emotions and reactions coming at her, no matter how strange or negative, and the things the patient does to her as 'the instrument', as depersonalised items to be wondered at and pored over in the light of all else that is known about the patient.

One of my supervisees and I struggled for weeks, trying to help him to get the right psychological distance between himself and his

patients. The writings he brought on the subject were headsplit-
tingly complicated and we got nowhere. Finally, in desperation, I
said: 'Think of your patient as an extra-terrestrial tomato. You
have never seen one before. Stare at it, wonder at it. Now find out
what it is *like*, not what it can do for you. Don't be needy: be
curious.' It helped a bit, though somewhat shocked by being asked
to see his patient as a tomato, he had to go away and think it over
first.

THE MUMSY SUPERVISEE

Like a loving mum, this supervisee finds it hard to stand her
patient's pain. She tends to reassure when she should interpret.
This does little harm and the patient feels better, but it does no
therapeutic good for he is none the wiser about himself. She has
robbed him of the chance to learn from his suffering, by shortening
the length of or reducing the intensity of that suffering.

This is not to say there is no room for reassurance or empathy
in psychotherapy. But it should be dispensed judiciously for the
patient's benefit, usually to help him contain unbearable hurt or
dread from one session to the next, rather than to gratify the
therapist's need to take the pain away.

A patient who has locked away hurt and misery for years may
cry his heart out during one phase of therapy. With the therapist
as attentive but non-invasive witness, such a catharsis can be im-
mensely healing. But if the therapist's anguished, damp-eyed face
shows him how moved she is, he may be unable to continue. If a
person needs to lose control for a bit, he needs to feel the witness
is very much *in* control.

Sometimes tears are produced by a patient instead of anger; he
has learned that this gets a more sympathetic response and avoids
possible rejection. The Mumsy therapist perpetuates this by never
challenging the tears, her need to protect and empathise being
stronger than her will to help him *understand* (and thus start to
vary) the behaviour. To get him to see why he always cries might
involve making him feel angry at *her* for not obliging him with the
expected empathic response. Unless she is prepared to be unpopu-
lar for a little while, how will he ever learn to constructively deploy
his assertiveness rather than his tears, to get his needs met?

If she can make it possible for him to express anger, experience
with her that as a result the roof did not fall in, he might begin to
realise that the price he pays for slipping in tears where anger

ought to be, is a continuation of low self-esteem and dependence. Does the supervisee really prefer for him a life of constant weeping and depression? Of course not. But the Mumsy Supervisee is rarely aware of what she is doing, until the supervisor shows her.

The Mumsy Supervisee has often had much sorrow in her own life. She understands suffering so well that she has a special talent for enabling patients to contact their pain and express it. The senior Mumsy Supervisee has become wise to her compulsion to comfort so lets the anguish continue unabated, but has to comfort still, by sharing in it. She is almost *comfortable* when her feelings are so close to another's pain. It may not be pleasant but it is familiar – and so safe – territory.

She is so absorbed by feeling, she can barely *think* about what is happening, continue with her analysing function as well as her supporting one. It is as if she draws all the hurt in a patient – has a valency for it – very fast, but in consequence misses out on some of the anger, joy, cruelty, vengefulness that he also contains, which needs airing equally, but with which she feels less at home. Therapists tend to find in their patients what they unconsciously want to find.

Perhaps her own hurt is recognised in the patient, to whom she then awards all the understanding and care she herself would have dearly loved. Something of this sort usually emerges in this supervisee's own therapy. That, however is private. The supervisor's concern is to help this supervisee, too, to find the optimal degree of emotional involvement with and distance from her patient.

The Mumsy Supervisee is extremely conscientious, with an overdetermined sense of responsibility. She usually takes on far too many patients, unable to bear them having to wait. She tends to go over time, grant extra sessions before fully thinking out the implications, and she is always the one who looks haggard long before a holiday is due, drained by trying single-handedly to water her patient's emotional deserts instead of helping them to get out and quench their own thirst.

THE ACADEMIC SUPERVISEE

The Academic Supervisee is in many ways the opposite of the Mumsy Supervisee. Where she is too close to feeling and finds it hard to think, the Academic Supervisee thinks constantly, perhaps as a way to defend against the possibility of being swamped by emotion.

The Academic Supervisee is sometimes precise to the point of obsessionality. In supervision she brings beautifully prepared – sometimes even typed! – notes on her sessions with the patient. As we go through them she will ask: 'Now just what sort of transference was that?' 'Is that what Freud meant by an anal fixation?' 'Was I being a Kleinian bad breast there?' 'Are we into the defence called reaction-formation here?'

Everything in the treatment must be sorted, labelled and boxed. She is driven to make tidy and classifiable what in the final analysis is an untidy and inexact business. She makes concrete and inviolable what are in fact concepts, notions and theories that are highly debatable, unprovable, constantly argued over and revised with each new generation in the light of new clinical evidence.

All the same, such a supervisee keeps her supervisor on her toes, asking her opinion of new authors or new research she has often never heard of. This supervisee will never need to be cautioned against sloppy technique or wild interventions. She is not without feelings, but does tend to keep them close to her chest. The supervisor needs to help her access them, assure her that untidy, illicit, negative feelings about a patient are just as potentially valuable as the 'correct' professional ones.

Such a supervisee is more vulnerable than she looks. Her search for exactness, her intellectuality, her inability to bear the *mystery* of psychotherapy (not to be confused with its muddle, which she can't stand either), can prove irritating to colleagues and supervisors. But it is important to realise that such a person may be trying to deal with enormous self-doubt, or fear of losing control, by so embracing academic certainty.

Supervisors are there to help supervisees in their work, just as therapists are there to treat patients. In neither case is the recipient of help under any obligation to be lovable! What *does* matter, very much, is whether a working/Therapeutic Alliance can be forged between them.

If the Academic Supervisee and the Mumsy Supervisee could trade some of their excesses with each other, they would make gifted therapists. This is one strong argument for group supervision. It is true that each participant has to share the supervisor and has less time to present cases, but she benefits greatly from seeing other supervisees at work, recognising their, and by comparison her own, positive and negative personality traits. Consciously, half consciously and unconsciously, imitative experiments in group participants' consulting rooms begin to happen; the hybridisation of approaches and techniques of ultimate benefit to the patients.

THE EGALITARIAN SUPERVISEE

This supervisee is high-principled, serious-minded, often with strong political, religious or philosophical views where the notion of equality is sacrosanct; all hierarchies and organisations wielding power being treated with great suspicion. Her rock-like integrity can sometimes make her seem humourless.

I have sometimes been brought up short by such a supervisee disapproving of some innocent (to me) joke about a patient, or my expression of exasperation, boredom or irritability with the patient's material. I take my personal reactions to material as grist to the clinical mill, but the Egalitarian Supervisee feels her patient is being attacked and must be defended.

A supervisee once told me about a patient on probation, who was only attending for treatment because of a court order. He came from an East End family of petty criminals always in and out of trouble, but clever and resourceful in their almost gleeful war with the police. I had the temerity to smile and call them 'a rum lot'. The supervisee was most upset, upbraided me for being a typical middle class, privileged, professional person who could afford to condescend because she had no idea what poverty and deprivation were about.

This was an extreme example of an Egalitarian Supervisee. More often, they go unnoticed until a particularly prejudiced patient gives them a hard time by forcing them to face a conflict between therapeutic and moral/political ideals. Such supervisees need to be helped to keep within the boundaries of psychotherapy and not use the treatment situation to convert or retrain the patient into 'better' attitudes.

The Egalitarian Supervisee is so concerned with not patronising her patient, she often gives him credit for knowledge, experience of the world, mature judgement that he does not possess. The supervisee is unwilling to make simple interventions lest she be guilty of insulting his intelligence. Consequently many of her patients are left bemused and frightened by her 'advanced' utterances. Neither would she dream of using what she sees as the condescending 'educative' GP to the Mind function, which can so often save a precarious therapy.

She is frequently in difficulty with the transference, finding it uncomfortable to be idealised, looked up to. She either fixes not to see it (denies it), the supervisor having to drag it out of her, or she overinterprets it, trying to shoo it away. Either way, she needs help to sit with the transference long enough to be able to study and *understand* it.

Regression is hard for this supervisee too. From time to time a patient may need to be a bit of a baby, the therapist a holding parent (usually mother). He may at other times regress to adolescence and his acting out has to be confronted by what he will experience as an authoritarian parent (usually father). The supervisee finds it hard to accept and work with her temporary role in this authority/dependency relationship, because she is too busy disapproving of it. In her world everybody is adult, equal and genderless.

For the Egalitarian Supervisee who seems not to respond to supervision, politicising and debating every suggestion made by the supervisor, more personal therapy is indicated, or even a change of career direction where her talents can be put to appropriate use.

This is not to deny that psychotherapy is a very political business. In our training courses, workshops and papers, the political dimension should regularly be considered. It has a place in supervision too, but not a dominating place.

THE MISSIONARY SUPERVISEE

The Missionary is never off duty. For her, psychotherapy is not just a psychological treatment, but a way of life, a religion even. She reads the latest therapy books, goes to all the open lectures, sits on committees to Get Things Done, socialises with other therapists – is quite possibly married to one, and at parties and pubs can always be found in intense discourse with someone about therapy. Her children and spouse may well be in therapy. Therapy can help everyone. Therapy is the Solution.

Underpinning this zeal is a belief that Mankind is perfectible. If only there was enough human-to-human love, communicating, sharing, after a good scrub out of the soiled contents of everybody's mind, the world would be Utopia. Such a supervisee loves her patients as well as wanting to treat them. She loves most those patients displaying loathsome behaviours and attitudes, because the rewards are that much higher when they are at last brought safely into the fold.

In supervision, problems arise when a patient holding similar assumptions about the world brings a depression that turns out to be a major collapse in just such a world view.

'All my life I let them (my parents) dictate to me. I went to a hateful school and never complained because of them. I went without a career so I could stay near to my poorly mother. I gave up my fiance because they didn't like him, I went to their church, not mine, year in year out. I never raised my voice, never had an opinion of my own. I was *good*. I loved them, honoured them. Now they are dead and I am on my own. I waited all that time for them to accept me, value me. They never did. *Where is my reward?*'

This patient's thinking had been similar to the Missionary's in that self-denial, dedicated service, the banishment of all anger and hate ought, in a fair world, to have earned her the love and recognition she so badly wanted from her parents. Love should breed love. Being good should make goodness come to her. She has found in midlife that all her cherished values counted for nothing. She has not been repaid in kind. She is now bitter, tearful, depressed, disillusioned. How could the world be this way?

Does the Missionary therapist adopt the attitude that her patient is depressed so is bound to see things as worse than they are? Does she intervene in suitably couched terms to the effect that virtue should be its own reward? Or that the patient will surely be rewarded in heaven? Does she, in therapy-speak, preach forgiveness? Any of these interventions (and I have had them all reported to me) sound to me like a continuation of the parental control from which the patient needs to be liberated.

Yet how can the Missionary, with her golden view of Mankind, encourage this patient to face that she is right, that the world can be a cruel place where the powerful exploit the meek, indoctrinate them with lies about goodness being repaid with love? How can she assist this patient to hate what has been done to her, when the supervisee herself cannot distinguish between inappropriate neurotic hate and the legitimate hate that comes with the realisation of one's exploitation, hate which after a period of bitterness and fury leads to self-reassessment and a new philosophy of life?

Real love and forgiveness (not the love and forgiving of which so many Missionaries blithely speak), is only attainable after a long struggle with negative, even murderous feelings, long denied in an attempt to appear just as loving and sharing as the Missionary would have us all be.

Learning to love, share and communicate isn't just a question of evacuating unwanted memories, feelings, beliefs and attitudes that stand in the way of the light, but of coming to appreciate how they got there, that *no wonder* they got there; of perhaps swinging then to an opposite extreme – anger where neediness was, hate where dependency was, rejection where there was enslavement.

Only when emotional exhaustion sets in, years of pain and rage having been finally freed from their prison, faced, then let go of or reintegrated, does the pendulum swing back, hover, then settle in a place the subject finds comfortable.

Too many therapists, especially Missionary ones, try to bypass the stage where they must get their hands dirty, participating in the drawing out of very negative feelings, even encouraging them. If they cannot bear hearing such thoughts and feelings, or voicing them themselves, how can the patient even dare admit them to consciousness? It is all too easy to censor a patient's productions, as easy as it is for a parent to wordlessly convey disapproval, or with a glance threaten withdrawal of love.

In the session it is not enough to talk *about* anger or hate; it needs to be *experienced* in the consulting room, in the calm and containing presence of the permissive therapist, who should have already faced her own demons in her own therapy.

Neither is it of much use to talk constantly about the past with a patient as if it were dead history, something that, granted, was nasty, but happened long ago. For the patient it happened yesterday or is happening now, re-enacted daily in his key relationships. The perpetrator is alive and active inside him, as is his own impotence and fear experienced at the time. A confrontation must occur between them if he is to get better. There is no Time, no 'distant past' in the unconscious.

In painting such a rosy picture of the world of psychotherapy, all nasty mess scraped up and conveniently discarded, leaving only the unalloyed glow of love, I wonder whether this supervisee is trying to tidy up her own unacceptable 'dirt'. The patient's grave doubts about and attacks on the world risk contaminating her own positive view, so these 'bad' feelings are regarded as invalid, bits of old muck clinging to an otherwise gleaming human being: the muck must be 'cleansed', cut away; not worked over and accepted, which is what I believe happens in proper therapy.

In good therapy there are just *feelings* – neither good nor bad – at various levels of awareness. 'Bad' was felt to be bad by the very young patient and so repressed, left for years to fester, rather than being brought into the fresh air from time to time to see if the feelings really were so wicked.

Rather than airing them, some Missionaries succeed in developing a mutually dependent relationship with patients where the hidden agenda is to aid one another's repression of 'wickedness' even further, while reinforcing one another's 'positiveness'. The Missionary becomes a benevolent despot; the patient has traded-in one overbearing parent for another. As in the original situation this manipulation of one human being by another masquerades as love.

The more extreme Missionaries make 'friends' with patients after treatment is over, sometimes setting up their own therapeutic schools, and/or 'alternative' communities, with their acolytes about them. The 'bad' qualities in members are then projected on to the external community who are seen at best as the pitiful non-enlightened, at worst as the spiritual enemy.

The Missionary, who for the time being can accept neither despair and hate in her patient, nor 'bad' feelings in herself, can be enormously helped by skilled supervision, though the work will stray often into that grey area between therapy and supervision.

Clearly it is important not to confuse the Missionary with supervisees displaying a wholesome hope and faith in psychodynamic psychotherapy and a healthy enthusiasm for work that we old 'uns might secretly envy!

THE CYNIC

The Cynic is in many ways diametrically opposed to the Missionary. Usually a senior therapist, always one with vast life experience, she doubts whether people can really change at all.

This may seem a surprising thing for a therapist to say, but then it all depends what is meant by 'change'. What the Cynic means is that though patients ostensibly get better, or better than they were when they came, it is only attitudes that have shifted, ways of processing incoming data that have been reorganised so that falling prey to transference is avoided. The therapeutic relationship itself has proved that quality relationships are possible and so, much former hopelessness has been lifted as well. But the fundamental personality *structure* remains the same. One is dealt a set of cards at birth. They cannot be changed or handed in. As a result of life's vicissitudes many cards get twisted and torn while others are left unused, until a therapist comes along, makes the patient pick up the whole pack and have a good shuffle, prior to a joint inspection. Her view is that therapy can only develop what potential – what 'cards', be they badly damaged or totally untried – are already there. She will work with any hand a patient has been dealt, realistic about possible outcomes.

This sober outlook enables the Cynic to take on patients whom other therapists have rejected as hopeless, and work what appear to be miracles (small miracles, but miracles nonetheless). The Cynic knows how slow, contrary, resistant to new learning a personality can be, but also what surprises it can come up with, provided the right 'card' – even if filthy and shredded – is lying about somewhere. And even if it isn't she will do what *is* do-able without complaint.

As she never expects too much from psychotherapy, accepting that we are still in the Dark Ages with regard to the discipline, she knows how to wait. She is grateful for any development that allows her to manoeuvre and she is not fussy what kind of patient she is asked to work with. She will have a go at most things, too life-experienced and self-attuned to require the patient to gratify her personal needs by producing material to her taste.

The Cynic was almost certainly once a great idealist, but time and experience have tempered her views. She has a tendency to make sardonic remarks: 'Psychotherapy – talk – is all we've got with which to help these people, so we might as well use it. But it's pretty primitive stuff when you think about it, isn't it?' Or, on being congratulated when an ex-patient, once on the threshold of suicide, is granted some high office: 'He would have got better anyway in the end.' When the supervisor comments on the excellent progress a patient is making: 'Basic behaviour modification with a smidgen of attitude retraining, that's all. We call it one thing, the other lot call it something else. Boils down to the same thing in the end, common sense.'

When a patient makes a good Alliance, the Cynic puts this down to his innate capacity – the 'Attachment' card dealt him at birth. But when the Alliance eludes her, the idealist in her rises to the surface and she struggles mightily to do the impossible. Because of her seniority she probably has many cases like this on her books. It is at times like these that she can become quite worried about her work, but will not burden the supervisor by bringing this up herself. The Cynic tends to appear emotionally self-sufficient, rarely refers to her private life or her past, and sees dealing with any personal distress about her work as her own responsibility. She often carries far too much internal stress as she detests 'whingeing'. The supervisor needs to be aware of this and to find some acceptable way to be supportive at such times.

Disguised, lengthy and undramatic depression is also common among Cynics, who will outwardly shrug it off as just one more 'given', about which nothing can be done, but who I suspect do value its having been noticed and uncritically commented on.

7 TEACHING PHILOSOPHY AND ETHICS THROUGH SUPERVISION (1)

Whenever I see or hear words like *philosophy* or *ethics* with regard to psychotherapy I find myself stifling a yawn while feeling guilty for so doing. *Of course* I know it is a vital subject: if we have no codes of practice, no agreed set of professional values, heaven help our patients, who stand to be abused without any course of redress. Yet the subject can seem tedious. No one enjoys being told how to behave properly, as if they could not work it out for themselves. No responsible therapist would have sexual relations with her patient; charge him exorbitant fees; experiment with his mind untrained and unsupervised for her own interest and/or gratification. Lectures from doughty tutors on ethics tend to be received as thinly-guarded insults or as worthy but rather embarrassing sermons.

In supervision though, ethical and clinical issues often combine, producing more interest and challenge to the supervisory couple. What to do, for instance, when the ethically right way to respond can feel clinically wrong or vice versa?

For example, a patient starting private therapy in the therapist's home might ask what she uses the room for outside working hours. From a clinical point of view the therapist knows that comments on the setting are virtually always about the therapist herself, so may want to explore the transference a bit further by inviting the patient to fantasise about what happens when he is out of the way. If I were supervising this therapist however, I would advise her to 'come clean'. Whatever else this new patient may be doing, he is looking for boundaries: is this session in this room a private sealed-off place and time for him or not? Until he feels that it is, he will be unable to relax or trust the therapist though he may go on producing pseudo material to keep her placated. Without the sense of safety his productions are valueless, except as defences against the invading therapist and whoever she represents.

I do not have a big house, so my study has to double as the waiting room. Patients can easily deduce its personal use from the desk, pinboard and word processor plus the odd holiday snap and pictures. I pondered long and deep over this and felt in the end that an ordinary human atmosphere was better than clinical white walls devoid of ornament.

But I *always* take any opportunity early on, to establish that the *consulting* room is exclusively for patients' use. I never enter it for any other purpose; there are no personal mementos in it; the furniture is always exactly the same. Implicit in this is the message: I am here in this session exclusively for you: this is *our* room.

Once a feeling of safety is established, comments on the setting can be associated to and analysed in the more 'clinically correct' way (unless the patient is regressing and in need of further assurance, or is reacting to some real break in the therapeutic frame by cueing the therapist to notice and hopefully repair it).

The provision, protection and maintenance of a safe psychological space for the patient is the very foundation of every treatment. Failure to establish such a space is about as morally desirable as a surgeon wielding a rusty scalpel. Associations can wait; dreams can wait; the patient's life story can wait. A broken frame must never wait.

Supervisees often believe there is only one 'correct' intervention. It is important to point out to them that for every intervention they do actually make, at least three or four other equally 'correct' ones probably exist. The art is in making the best choice. In the above case reassurance (so often given at the wrong time) was specifically employed to secure the frame and to avoid unethical conduct. The gain from creating trust and providing safety was deemed more important than the loss of transferential material or a chance to interpret.

Inherent in the philosophy of dynamic therapy is the idea that an intervention designed to do a specific job – linking; frame maintenance; promotion of catharsis; slowing or speeding up the material; shedding light; drawing or interpreting the transference – to mention but a few – is better than the one that is most clever, most deep, most exposing of the patient's inner conflicts irrespective of timing, or giving most opportunity for the therapist to show off. Always the intervention is made (or deliberately held back) with the patient's current state of vulnerability/resilience in mind as well as the present state of the Therapeutic Alliance.

Most philosophical and ethical issues that come to supervision do so accidentally. The supervisee brings clinical material that reveals ethical issues she had not known were there; it is the supervisor who spots them. A common example is that of the supervisee anxious to know if some interpretation she made was 'right'. From an ethical point of view she needs help to see that being right is not the only thing that counts. She must always consider her patient's state of mind *at that particular moment* before speaking her thoughts. She needs a sense of how much insight he can take at one go, how far the pair are through this particular session so there will be time to deal with any reaction to the interpretation, and how the patient reacted to similar interpretations before.

Should the intervention be made with solemnity or humour? Should it be a gentle hint or a confident announcement? Should it be simple, left for the patient to tease out for himself, or elaborated so that he is left in no doubt of its importance to his situation? Making interpretations, no matter how theoretically sound, without this background awareness is as dangerous in psychological terms as the person driving a powerful sports car without attention to the speed limit or traffic conditions.

Generally speaking, supervisees are genuinely ignorant of any wrong doing but have to be helped to understand their recklessness – or indeed their inappropriate reservation when they fail to tackle or even recognise material crying out for comment.

I have never met a supervisee who would deliberately injure a patient, but many do unwitting harm when their behaviour, and more importantly the *motive* for their behaviour, is not checked by the supervisor. It is these *unconscious* abuses of the therapist's position that are so potentially damaging; for the patient – who may or may not have unconsciously solicited or colluded in the abuse – is all too often unaware it is happening, so cannot complain.

Every unintentional abuse by therapists cannot be satisfactorily lectured about on a course because they are idiosyncratic to each practitioner. Every therapist has her own personality quirks making her more susceptible to certain unethical acts and attitudes than others. In a long supervisory relationship the supervisee makes the same inadvertent errors over and over again, though they may be so subtle as to go unnoticed for a long time. When the supervisor comes to know her supervisee well, she can predict and often avert unethical activity.

This highlights once again the limited value of the one off, casual supervision session. In the intimate and trusting environment of regular supervision, which mirrors the regular therapeutic space provided for her patient by the supervisee, all unwitting abuses and exploitations can be illumined and corrected, and a more wholesome philosophy worked for.

I shall explore some of the more common ethical problems that arrive in supervision by listing a series of dos and don'ts for the supervisee, which are not substitutes for supervision, but might assist the supervisee to recognise more quickly situations that need supervision. Readers who are supervisors might remind themselves through these vignettes and anecdotes just how vital a part they have to play in raising ethical awareness as well as clinical skill in their supervisees.

NEVER UNDERESTIMATE YOUR IMPORTANCE TO THE PATIENT

Analogies between the therapist's work and the parent's are so often drawn they can seem cliched, banal. But over and above a specific patient's positive or negative parental transference to a particular therapist, is another more general process of attachment that, except in the most damaged patient, might be described as a human 'given', a characteristic shared by us all. As surely as monkeys make for the bananas, moths make for the flame and cats mark out with scent their territorial borders, so do humans attach themselves to other humans – 'no man is an island ...' People who feel lost or in pain or uncertain will attach more readily than most and will often hang on to even the most toxic relationship, be it with a therapist or anyone else, despite all the evidence of unwholesomeness.

As Judith Viorst says in *Necessary Losses* (1986, chapter 1, p. 22):

> It doesn't seem to matter what kind of mother the child has lost, or how perilous it may be to dwell in her presence. It doesn't matter whether she hurts or hugs. Separation from mother is worse than being in her arms when the bombs are exploding. Separation from mother is sometimes worse than being with her when she is the bomb.

The separation from and loss of first attachment figures is not restricted to 'neurotic' people' *it is a universal human experience.* To develop and grow, every person has to come to terms with separation, accept the uncomfortable realisation that ultimately they are alone in the world; they were born alone and will die alone, no matter who else is present at the time.

Though independence has its obvious advantages, all of us at low times consciously or unconsciously long for reattachment, that state of togetherness that can create the illusion, if only for a while, that we are loved and protected unconditionally and eternally. It is the main drive, in combination with the sexual one, that makes us 'marry in haste and repent at leisure', that made possible the joke about a second marriage being 'the triumph of hope over experience'. The need to 'settle down' so often disguises a wish to regress and be looked after, no matter what the price.

Anyone dedicating time and money to psychotherapeutic treatment is likely to be in a low state and therefore highly susceptible to any offer of attachment made by the therapist, *even if his symptoms are not linked to a particular parent*. It follows therefore that therapists' holidays, illnesses and absences are of tremendous import and their possible psychological effects on the patient should never be overlooked. It is not personal conceit but good ethical practice to remind and prepare a patient for the therapist's breaks regularly and often. This applies to all patients, not just those the therapist feels have a parental transference to her.

Case Example

A young psychiatrist unexpectedly had to change hospitals as the nature of his post had been altered. It was now split between clinical work and the department's new research project, all of which took place in a different unit. This meant that he had to write to some six or seven patients he had seen for Assessment and explain that another psychiatrist would have to finish the job on his behalf. In the letter he enclosed an appointment with the new doctor, apologising for any inconvenience caused.

Inconvenience was the least of his problems. Though his consultant had assured him that he had handled the changeover correctly, he still felt vaguely guilty. A week later the new psychiatrist rang him at home in a very agitated state because one of these patients had overdosed the night before her new appointment.

It became clear in supervision that this patient, who had seen several therapists already, had finally been able to put her trust in my supervisee. With a history of foster parents and children's homes, the sudden changeover was seen as another in a long line of rejections and her attempt at suicide (she almost succeeded) was her angry and despairing reaction.

My supervisee initiated a mutual consultation with the new psychiatrist about which the patient was told, when she recovered enough to return to treatment. This was a damage-limitation exercise, in that the patient felt slightly less abandoned knowing her original doctor had at least talked things over with his successor and so seemed to be taking a bit of care over her fate.

My supervisee was terribly shocked by the whole episode, as he had only seen the patient twice. He could not believe that in so short a time he had come to mean so much to her.

DO NOT ABUSE THE PATIENT WITH YOUR OWN NARCISSISM

We have all seen patients who make us feel it is the parent who should be in therapy, not the offspring. Alas, as a supervisor I have seen many therapists who should be in treatment rather than, or as well as, their patient.

Like the self-centred and/or overly ambitious parent, some therapists see their patients as walking advertisements for their skill and talent and so need them very badly to get well quickly, no matter how disabled they may be or feel. Keen therapists often forget they are there to develop and heal the patient *to his greatest capacity* – which may be very limited – not to glorify their own reputation with a string of successes.

Case Example

Dawn was a student counsellor in a university. She had seen Erik, a second-year classics undergraduate for a term, i.e. ten sessions.

Her excellent Dynamic Formulation, which she had made in the first session was: 'A potential candidate for first-class honours, this socially and sexually underconfident young man is doing no work, following a break up with his first serious girlfriend who became fed up with his intermittent impotence. She represented for him his possessive mother who, in grooming him for academic stardom and discouraging all friendships especially with girls, made him acutely anxious about 'performance'. His current inability (refusal?) to study seems to be a combination of rebellion against the actual mother's stress on academic matters, and a real fear of failing to match up academically as he has failed sexually. His father is no help to him as he dotes on Erik's younger sister who has Down's syndrome and of whom Erik has always been envious, yet guilty about his envy because of her low intelligence, where his is supposedly so high. Eager to work, and able to understand interpretation, these maturational problems should respond well to psychotherapy.'

Erik did indeed respond well, but Dawn was very worried because he wanted to leave at the end of term. 'There's so much work still to do', she protested in supervision. 'How can I get him to see he has still not begun to deal with his sister, and how do we know he won't be impotent again with the new girlfriend?'

'Is that why he wants to terminate, because he's in love?' I asked.

'Yes.'

'And maybe like his mum, you are feeling possessive, want to groom him for therapeutic stardom the way she coached him academically?'

'But the sister, and the disappointment in father, and the sexual failure. All our work so far has focussed on mother alone. We haven't finished!'

'Well,' I said, 'it sounds as if he has. He's done what he came to do, get angry with and emotionally separate from mum: the rest he'll learn about through experience. How old is he?'

'Nineteen and a bit.'

'And where is his family?'

'Dundee.'

When conducting psychotherapy, do be aware always of the patient's developmental stage. This young man in the first flush of sexual activity has plenty of time and opportunity to find his potency for himself. Already he has a new girlfriend and is optimistic. Should there be difficulties he can always return to therapy. As for working with the topic of his family, it might well be rather late, as they are at the other end of the country and he is psychologically moving away from home too. This area is unresolved, yes, but is no longer therapeutically 'hot'. For the moment he has better fish to fry. When a patient falls in love, you cannot fight it. You sit it out or let him go.

An older patient, say a middle-aged man with similar sexual and work problems, might well have wanted to stay in therapy longer, might feel more ready to deal with the internalised family that still dogs his tracks. It is the patient's clinical agenda that counts, not the therapist's. Many people can only do a bit at a time, and you should bear in mind always that you are not the only therapist in the world.

The need to keep Erik in treatment spoke eloquently of Dawn's *desire to have a star patient to reflect her abilities in an academic community where tutors were still suspicious about the whole counselling business. It was also a counter-transference on her part; like Erik's mother, she could not let him go, especially to a rival.*

Erik got his first-class honours degree, kept the second girlfriend, and never returned to the counselling service.

This case shows again how intertwined clinical and ethical issues are. It has to be accepted though, that some patients threatening or actually leaving treatment *are* acting out and need help to see this, but such an explanation is all too often offered as a justification for the therapist hanging on to a favourite patient.

DO RESPECT THE PATIENT'S DEFENCES

Whilst no therapist would do this on purpose, stealing a patient's defences by prematurely interpreting them leads either to breakdown and/or total dependency on the therapist. Now she has power, authority, control. The patient desperately needs her. Stripped of his own coping mechanisms he must rely on her absolutely, believe her every word, be guided by her in all things. She may feel important and see this attachment as 'positive transference' or 'necessary regression', when it is no such thing. It constitutes a highly unethical exploitation of the patient's trust, and must be tackled immediately it appears in supervision.

Case Example

Michael was a doctor working in an NHS outpatient psychotherapy clinic. His patient, Ronald, was a 46-year-old senior research scientist at a nuclear power station. A year ago his wife, on whom he had greatly depended all their married life, had died of cancer, since which time he had become increasingly morose, unmotivated to feed or wash himself or go out. He managed a bath once a fortnight and lived mainly on toast and baked beans. His clothes were now scruffy and unironed, his face badly in need of a shave. Work seemed the only thing that kept him going. He was doing the most creative work he had ever done, writing furiously, thinking out technical problems late into the night and again when he woke at five in the morning. But his employer had become worried by his increasing eccentricity, and in the end insisted he see a psychiatrist.

The psychiatrist, Michael, was an enthusiastic proponent of short-term focal therapy. His consultant had done Ronald's Assessment, located the focus as 'inability to mourn', and had accordingly briefed Michael to treat Ronald in 12 sessions. A proper Assessment would have shown that Ronald needed a much slower approach, and that the so-called mourning problem was but the tip of the iceberg.

Michael had got to session nine and was panicking that the patient was so 'regressed' he feared he would never get him on his feet in the three remaining sessions. Afraid to face his consultant with failure, Michael got my name from a colleague and contacted me privately.

Michael's short-term approach was rather structured. He always took a full case-history in the first session, but in this case at least never seemed to use it again. I had him take me through the history and it emerged that Ronald had been brought up by a remote, affluent, scientist father who never noticed him and a gentle, servile mother who waited on him hand and foot. Ronald loved schoolwork but seemed uninterested in making friends. His childhood seemed a contented but uneventful time.

Mum visited Ronald every weekend at university, bringing food parcels and fresh shirts. At 30 he met Sally, his wife, who had been sexually abused by her uncle and was uninterested in sex. As Ronald had no experience either, and wanted none, they were drawn together in mutual relief and married a year later, whereupon Sally took over from where mum, now arthritic, left off.

Ronald became quite famous in his professional circle and was always going to international conferences and high-level meetings. Sally did all the organising, travelling with him everywhere, ensuring he had all he needed so that no distraction from his work would be necessary. In short, this man had never experienced independence or conscious discomfort in his whole life. He was as helpless as a baby.

Michael, it seemed to me, relentlessly interpreted Ronald's work as a defence against grief, making him feel insecure about the one and only thing in his life that was working well. It was but a compensation, urged Michael; he should be making space for the grief, not denying it. He suggested Ronald should stop the early morning work and instead, when he couldn't sleep, give over the time to memories of happy times with Sally to see if this might uncork the grief. Ronald did as he was told. Michael said that Ronald should get out more, join a club. Ronald tried and failed, scared by the liveliness of others. This depressed him further. Michael interpreted Ronald's scruffy demeanour as unconscious anger with his wife for leaving him: 'Look what

you have done to me.' It was no good denying anger, he kept insist-
ing, it was a part of normal mourning and together they would get it
all into the open. He then suggested Ronald should bring in a photo
album with Sally's picture in it. This did the trick all right. Ronald
wept as he had never wept since Sally died. Michael was pleased and
encouraged more catharsis.

By now Ronald had lost all confidence in his work, seeing it
(taught by Michael) as a coward's way out. Having failed to make
new friends and possessing none from the past, his doctor became
the protector, adviser, manager and support that his mother and
wife had been. Michael felt the patient was leech-like in his de-
pendency and was becoming uncomfortable where formerly he had
felt flattered. Now the patient had started ringing him at home and
asking for extra sessions.

Supervision consisted first in me controlling my angry feelings
about the mismanagement of the case, then teaching Michael
something about the critical nature of Assessment (this one had
been deeply inadequate). I tried to help him to see how important
it is to let transference develop at a manageable pace for both
parties, rather than cultivating it, then being overwhelmed by it,
then blaming the patient for its now inconvenient existence. I tried
to explain how 'stuck' grieving is itself an adaptive, necessary cop-
ing defence which has to be dismantled gently, a bit at a time, in
a calm containing environment, without stimulation, suggestion
and interpretation always intruding.

Last but by no means least, I impressed upon him how unethi-
cal and against the basic philosophy of dynamic therapy, was any
idea that kicking out defences from under a patient, so forcing
entry into the domain of grief, could ever be justified. Michael had
genuinely but mistakenly believed he was helping the patient.

I packed off a very nervous Michael to negotiate an extension
with his consultant, who in the event allowed him six more ses-
sions. I continued to supervise the case and helped Michael to
arrange subsequent private therapy for Ronald (courtesy of his past
earnings that Sally had wisely invested in shares).

DO NOT SEDUCE OR BE SEDUCED

A patient unhappy with his therapist often solicits help from another. Whether or not the original therapist is at fault, it is important that the newly-approached therapist does not steal the patient,
or give in to seductive appeals from the patient to rescue him.

I once heard through a colleague, of a therapist alleged to have eaten cream buns in his sessions with an anorexic patient, who not unsurprisingly wondered if she should change therapists. Even in such appalling conditions as these, it is essential that the patient has the complaint out with the therapist concerned and makes an ending of the current treatment before starting a new one.

In many circumstances there has been a genuine misunderstanding which can be cleared up if the patient is encouraged to share his feelings of doubt and disappointment with the offending therapist. On other occasions a very powerful transference makes the patient helplessly act out his anger with, or fear of, his therapist by finding a new one. And it has to be admitted that some therapists, like the one above, really are beyond the pale and must be stood up to. Newly-approached therapists may not be able to judge what has gone before, but should avoid aiding and abetting acting out, or depriving the patient of a chance to have a necessary showdown that proves to him that he is perfectly capable of standing up to a powerful figure without crumbling. The second therapist can offer valuable support to help him take this step.

Sometimes the patient plays an active part in these triangular situations. 'I am sure *you* can help me, you are so much more senior/well known/understanding/less doctrinaire than my own therapist.' Flattered, the new therapist agrees to take him on and just assumes the old arrangement has been terminated.

On occasion it can be hard to know who is seducing whom; but there is no doubt that while a patient is entitled to express his problems his own way, for as yet he does not understand what he is unconsciously doing, so has no choice, the therapist has no right whatever to react subjectively, but must at all times view the behaviour of the patient in a psychodynamic, professional light. The first therapist must be enabled by the second to reunite with her hostile patient (i.e. he is sent straight back), and to help him analyse the meaning behind this attempt to change therapists. If the patient is still not satisfied, he is at liberty to end treatment and seek a new therapist.

In the early stages of training (if the course is any good) the question of attire, language and touch as potential seduction is always addressed. I have had supervisees of both sexes sporting nose studs, ear rings, bovver boots, jumble-sale outfits my granny might have worn, slashed and fraying jeans, miniskirts fit to give a girl pneumonia, up-to-the-minute designer clothes that look impossible to feel comfortable in for 50 minutes, skinheads, pinkheads and dreadlocks and a truly amazing assortment of hats. (It always fascinates me why anyone would want to participate in supervision wearing a hat, but then I am old fashioned.) Though not all of these outfits accorded with my taste I tried to imagine the 'client group'. A therapist would hardly wear a city suit and tie if he wished to win the regard of rebellious youngsters, though it can be argued that perhaps he should not dress in a manner totally atypical of him either, for that would be trying to pull the wool over his patients' eyes.

It is sartorial *consistency* that matters more than sobriety. A therapist sticking to a particular style of dress, no matter how strange, is soon adjusted to, but the patient is thrown into confusion when, say, a female therapist who has turned up in jeans and shirts for six months, suddenly appears powdered and perfumed, in a clingy, short dress.

I had a male colleague once who rode to his day centre for the chronically mentally ill on his ancient bicycle, wearing baggy and stained corduroys and open sandals, but kept appointments with patients at the private clinic where he also worked in a smart suit and driving his red Porsche. During one particularly busy period he got his diary mixed up and arrived at the clinic to be redirected by his secretary to the day centre where a patient was already waiting for him. A group of day centre members hanging round the entrance smoking when he roared up in his Porsche could scarcely believe their eyes. My colleague was teased mercilessly for weeks afterwards by the members, but those he was seeing for individual therapy were deeply dismayed by or angry at the deception.

Patients often display a wish to seduce by the way they dress, talk, or try to touch. They are enacting their needs and conflicts in the only way they know how and the behaviour is a matter for discussion or interpretation at the right time. The therapist however should be under no illusion that she can expect equal rights in this regard. She jolly well ought to know her own needs and conflicts in this area as a result of her training and her own therapy, and not visit them upon the patient.

Playing out such preoccupations with a patient cannot be justified, and must in supervision be confronted. This is far from easy for there are very few supervisees who walk into their supervisor's office and announce that they tried to seduce their patient yesterday. As most of such behaviour is unconscious it is for the supervisor to bring up her suspicions and then treat the matter with firmness and tact.

A special mention should be made here of patients who have been sexually abused. All aspects of the therapist's personal presentation, the setting she provides, as well as the verbal detail (including tone of voice) of interventions should be carefully scanned, by the therapist herself as the session is occurring and afterwards in supervision. I supervised a young male therapist some years back, before sexual abuse was so much in the public eye, and he just could not understand why his female patient 'freaked out' at his locking the door! 'After all, I explained it was to prevent our being interrupted. I was only maintaining therapeutic boundaries.'

Many patients of both sexes have made seduction into a fine art. Though it has brought them little reward in terms of personal happiness, they are compelled to continue with it in therapy. They can flatter and cajole, tease and flirt in most disarming ways. The therapist is often not quite sure if she is imagining things. In supervision she can talk about such incidents – often very subtle – against the background of all the other material at her disposal and make a shared assessment of the behaviour with her supervisor. No matter how arousing or how distasteful it is, the behaviour needs to be treated as one symptom among others, and as such is in need of decoding. There is no advantage in being coy or embarrassed about it in supervision. And there is certainly no value in hoping that it will, with time, just go away.

One of the commonest forms of therapist seduction is that of making implicit promises to the patient that are impossible to keep. 'Stay with me, trust me, talk to me. I will be better than your mother ever was. I will make everything better.' Or: 'Never mind your broken love affairs. I will be your soulmate, feel your pain, think your thoughts with you, divine your needs and meet them.' Such a highly dangerous and unethical attitude is often only detectable by the supervisor when she asks for an 'action replay', invites the supervisee to make again the intervention she made in the session, using the same voice. The supervisor also counts the number of 'positive' interventions in the reported session, while calculating how many (or few!) of the interventions are designed to help the patient see the unpalatable truth of his situation. Where the supervisee is seducing the patient the former far outweigh the latter.

Any microscopic examination of a five-minute section of the session is likely to reveal this type of behaviour, which is why the supervisory sessions should be varied, sometimes concentrating on an overview of the whole treatment, sometimes focussing on one especially significant session and at other times spending the whole time just looking at one intervention.

Seductive behaviour on the part of the supervisee is often rational-ised as 'promoting the Alliance'. Making a Therapeutic Alliance has nothing to do with lulling the patient into a false sense of security and thereby adding another traumatic disappointment to his existing problems.

Case Example

Geraldine, my supervisee, worked in a community centre for ex-psychiatric patients. It was staffed mainly by volunteers, whom she was employed to support and train, and so spent much of her time in the community room with colleagues and ex-patients. However, her job also entailed a few counselling hours a week, for which a separate room was set aside.

Her little band of five devoted followers were nicknamed 'Ger-aldine's Groupies' by the other users of the centre. Doubtless this reflected some envy on their part, but they were also uneasily reacting to the way she blurred the boundary between her 'com-munity' work and her individual counselling. She sent postcards to her five patients whenever she took leave, brought them gifts on their birthdays, phoned them whenever they failed to 'drop in' at the centre on a non-counselling day, and when working in the community room tended to single them out for special projects – a picnic, a cooking session, a board game.

When I raised the boundary issue she protested that these were very damaged people; you couldn't get them to look at their unconscious. They wouldn't understand. Support and care had to be concrete, not just verbal. I could see her point if she were talking about the supportive work going on in the commu-nity room. Other members and volunteers sent cards and rang one another, and baked birthday cakes. It was part of the cul-ture. But in offering a separate counselling service she was surely trying to do something rather different? Hadn't the five been carefully selected by the head of the community as being suited 'in a limited way' to psychotherapy? All she seemed to be doing was seducing them into an overly dependent relationship which promised them a second mother – a promise she could not possibly keep, for she would leave one day, having failed to assist them to understand their inner world and thus develop whatever autonomy they were capable of. Drugging patients with emo-tional gratification can never substitute for real psychotherapy.

DO NOT USE BAD LANGUAGE

Providing it is not offensive or totally alien to the therapist, she might, with certain patients, adopt their vocabulary to make them feel more at ease with her and to improve communication flow. In that sense 'bad language' can be most helpful.

I remember a couple I was assessing many years ago, when I was still somewhat prissy and professional about my language. The husband was having trouble with penetrative sex and his wife was complaining of how frustrated she was getting. I delicately raised the possibility of oral or manual stimulation as a route to orgasm. The husband stared at me blankly.

'Harry, she means your fingers and your mouth, to make me come.'

Harry glared at me: 'Well why didn't you ruddy well say so?'

As soon as I started speaking English as they spoke it, the therapy fairly whistled along.

There is another kind of bad language – 'psychospeak' – frequently deployed in psychotherapy to cover up the therapist's uncertainty, to put the patient firmly in his place, or to impress upon him the unending wisdom of his therapist. Technical terms should always be avoided; why should an engineer or coal miner be expected to have heard of such things as transference, cathexis or projection, let alone understand them? How much do *you* know about engineering?

All professions have their own terminologies so that colleagues can discuss matters with each other in efficient 'shorthand'. To assume the patient should be able to 'speak the lingo' too, or to treat him as 'thick' because he doesn't catch your meaning at once is downright unfair. If an interpretation cannot be made in plain English, better not interpret at all.

Similarly, never use 'bad' language like *sado-masochistic*. Why not say instead: 'You only seem to know where you are in relationships if you are either the victim or the victor – nothing in between.'

Better describe a patient as being *needy* not *greedy*.

Rather than say: 'Your father was *mad*', (thus implying there is nothing the patient can do about it, except blame) why not say: 'It sounds as if his thinking and feeling were in different compartments most of the time, so he couldn't be "with you" in the way you needed', or perhaps: 'If that is how he was it's no wonder you've come to distrust your own judgement.'

It is often helpful too, to point out the patient's own 'bad' language, terms that spring automatically to his tongue and which always leave him in bad odour with himself: 'It's all my fault' (whether it is or not); 'I'm evil' (not 'I'm miserable/angry'); 'I deserve to be punished' (not 'I ought to be understood').

Sometimes a therapy is too short, or the patient cannot remember enough of the past, to make a neat Dynamic Formulation. Often a patient will significantly improve though, just through showing him how his defence mechanisms work, as they operate *in vivo* with the therapist, and getting him to reframe 'bad' statements about himself in a less damning way. Changing language can go some way to changing attitudes. This is one area where psychodynamic work and cognitive therapy have much in common.

ALWAYS DO A PROPER ASSESSMENT

Sometimes the Assessment has to *be* the therapy because so few sessions are available. If the patient leaves after a short time with some understanding of what the therapist calls the Dynamic Formulation, he will take away tools to work with. This means he will fare much better than the patient who is subjected to 'support' or 'just listening' and then abandoned. Shortage of time should not mean wastage of time.

The truly supportive approach should only be used after it has been recommended following a careful Assessment that has shown the unsuitability of this patient for even a modified dynamic approach. There exists real, profitable supportive work which has its own set of skills but which many dynamic therapists regard, wrongly, as inferior and amateurish. Then there is 'supportive therapy' which is all too often prescribed when either no one knows what to do, or the patient has been deemed untreatable but no one dare say so outright. This fudging may save face but helps no one, least of all the patient.

A rushed Assessment *can* be got away with if afterwards the patient is not too ill or low to cooperate in what is now an unnecessarily drawn-out process of finding 'the real problem', that is, the meaning of the symptoms and to what underlying conflict they represent a solution (albeit a solution that is no longer working effectively – why else has he come into treatment?) If he is too ill or low to cooperate though, he will be deprived of the additional or alternative treatment he has all along needed, and will get worse while the therapist wanders about without focus or aim. I have lost count of the times in supervision when I have had to take an 'advanced' therapy right back to basics, assist the supervisee to find the Dynamic Formulation she should have arrived at months, and sometimes even years ago.

In addition to saving time, money and a worsening of symptoms, a thorough Assessment allows the therapist freedom to manoeuvre – a chance to ask questions, have a 'real' conversation with the patient, draw up a psychological as well as factual history of him that throws light on his reactions to the present situation – that she will never enjoy again, once post-Assessment treatment has commenced. On the patient's side it is an opportunity to get the 'feel' of the human being into whose hands he is considering placing himself, learn to trust her, to ask her things that later on will not be answered, only interpreted: in short, to build that all important Alliance.

The clinical supervisor must always be aware that her supervisee's work takes place in a professional setting that can have a profound effect, good and bad, on the supervisee's work. Helping the supervisee to critically assess her work environment is just as important as aiding her to study the session itself.

Case Example

Jade was a community psychiatric nurse working in a new mental health team of three nurses, two social workers, a rehabilitation officer, an occupational therapist, two psychiatrists and a consult-ant psychiatrist. She had taken a two-year postgraduate training in psychodynamic counselling, as had the senior nurse who officially supervised her. Although she respected her senior colleague she grumbled that it was the blind leading the blind because they both had the same amount of experience and training.

Jade came to see me for three sessions of supervision after she and her senior had negotiated the necessary finances with the team as a whole. The position of team leader rotated annually but the first incumbent by common consent was the consultant. (This demonstrated a clinging to old organisational forms despite the 'new' team approach.)

Before she told me about the patient I asked Jade to give me a summary of how the team worked and why she had felt the need to demand money from the training budget. She had not so far struck me as the demanding type, but presented rather as stressed, frightened and professionally out of control.

Referrals came from GPs to a weekly 'allocation meeting' chaired by the consultant in his capacity as team leader. The idea was that personnel should volunteer their services to any patient they felt came into their area of expertise, after which a treatment package, maybe involving more than one team member, was drawn up and approved by the rest. In practice though, all bowed to the consultant's opinion. He was a 'decent sort of chap', very fair, very experienced, but not at all psychodynamic in outlook. By common consent he 'assessed' all new patients in a one-hour session before presenting them to the allocation meeting.

He had summed up Mrs Dixon as: 'A jobless widow of 40 with a chronic anxiety state, dependent on Valium for 15 years, needs weaning off.' All the other nurses were full and Jade, though she had but one short-term (ten sessions) vacancy, felt obliged to 'volunteer'. The consultant said that after five sessions he would reduce the patient's Valium, and then reduce it again at the end of therapy, before sending her back to the GP with the recommendation that the gradual reduction of the dose be continued. As she was lonely and jobless the occupational therapist offered her services and all agreed this to be a good thing.

Mrs Dixon's fate had been sealed without any proper Assessment, merely a diagnosis, which told very little about the patient's therapeutic needs.

Jade was at first much encouraged, for despite her anxiety and evident depression the patient seemed to respond warmly and quickly and could absorb and discuss animatedly all Jade's observations. By session five she agreed to a reduction in the Valium and felt very happy that for the first time in years she was able to consider this, thanks to the relationship with Jade.

Alas, this, unsurprisingly, was but a 'transference cure'. By session six Mrs Dixon was having panic attacks almost daily and was very physically agitated. Jade raised the possibility that this was not just because the pills had been reduced, but because the end of the therapy was in sight. Mrs Dixon said this was all too true, but what could she do about it? In four weeks time she'd be left to her own devices, which undoubtedly meant going back to her old dose of Valium. This threat, Jade saw as Mrs Dixon's (justifiable) rage at the powers that be, for giving with one hand and taking away with the other, just as her mother had done. Again Mrs Dixon agreed. Again she wailed: 'But what can I do about it? I've never been able to cope. My supports have always been cut from under my feet, just like now!'

By session eight Jade was feeling very panicky about the treatment. She saw the consultant, who after much persuasion, agreed to extend the therapy to 15 sessions, leaving another patient to languish on the waiting list. She also pleaded for some external supervision with me, as both she and her nurse supervisor felt the patient might become suicidal and they wanted a second opinion.

With the offer of more sessions Mrs Dixon calmed down and continued with the reduced dose of Valium. She did much work on her relationship with a very fickle mother whose giving one minute and taking away another left her hopelessly insecure and afraid to tackle any project with confidence.

In my first supervision session I asked about the dead husband (I always like to have an overview and he was conspicuously absent from Jade's account). Mrs Dixon had hardly discussed him, being overly preoccupied with her frightening physical symptoms and then memories of her mother. Jade went back and at an appropriate moment asked her to say something about him.

Mr Dixon had been killed in a road accident 15 years ago when for the first time in her marriage Mrs Dixon had considered an affair. The husband had been 'blow hot, blow cold' like her mother. After five years of marriage she began to feel angry and cheated. She met a man at work who seemed kind and loving and they started having lunch together.

When the manfriend, a divorcee, said he wanted to spend the rest of his life with her, no half measures, she could hardly believe it. Real commitment at last. Relations with her husband, a long-distance lorry driver, had become particularly strained in recent months and an affair was very tempting. She had been at the man's flat drinking wine at the very moment her husband was killed. Telling Jade this she wept and wept, calling herself a harlot and adulteress.

The roots of Mrs Dixon's problem lay in childhood, but to deal with so vast an area in so short a time was asking the impossible. If ten sessions were all that were available, Jade would have been better advised to concentrate on feelings over the husband's death, the similarity between the therapeutically 'hot' rage at and guilt over him, and the more denied, therefore therapeutically 'cool' rage and guilt over her mother, whom she had often wished dead and then prayed to God to punish her for having entertained such vile thoughts. Making this link would soon 'heat up' the old hurts and make them available for brief analysis.

The punishment that Mrs Dixon had all her life awaited, finally arrived in the form of her husband's fatal accident. (Doubtless he too had often been wished dead.) Adequate Assessment would have established at once that the Valium was first prescribed at the time of maximum guilt (diagnosed as 'anxiety state') so the focus of any

*therapy aimed at eventually getting her off the drug was bound to
be some kind of link between husband and mother.*

*In the time that remained for supervision, Jade and I decided on
a focus for ending. Now that Jade too, was going to 'ditch' the
patient, she would use Mrs Dixon's feelings about this to lead her
into feelings about being cheated all her life – as a child, as a wife,
and as potential mistress. We guessed and were proved right that
Mrs Dixon would become very angry at last about having to spurn
the one man in her life who might have made her happy (he had
subsequently married someone else) because of her useless guilt
over her husband and mother. She realised, as both Jade and I had
hoped, that for 15 years she had been placating her guilty conscience by drugging the unapproved-of rage, a rage to which in fact
she had every right: the drugs had to go.*

*The patient was returned to the GP and at my suggestion Jade
insisted on writing the report herself as she had been the therapist,
not the consultant. She presented a clear Dynamic Formulation of
what lay behind the addiction, along the lines above, and recommended the patient be referred to the local hospital's outpatient
psychotherapy clinic, despite the one-year waiting list. She offered
to see the patient every two months to tide her over.*

The 'hot' issue here was missed in the initial session, conducted by a general psychiatrist whose thinking was diagnosis-
and management-oriented, rather than psychodynamic. The psychiatric nurse deputed to treat the patient was given no chance
to make her own Assessment and then recommend an appropriate length of, and focus for, treatment, which with adequate
supervision she was perfectly capable of doing. The patient was
anxious, depressed and drug addicted to start with. By the time
her allocated time passed the half-way mark, the threat of termination had made her suicidal as well. Is this really the way we
want to treat patients?

DO NOT ABANDON

Mrs Dixon, above, clearly felt abandoned, having for the first time in
years made a good relationship which in time would have undoubtedly helped her to come off medication. True, no one meant or
wanted to abandon her, but that is no excuse for unethical management of a case. A good Assessment would have either awarded her
the length of therapy she needed (I've never in my life cured an

addiction in ten sessions and would not even attempt to), or granted her ten sessions *to work on the specific focus described above*, with a view to dealing medically with the addiction later, when she was referred for longer-term work with someone who would not abandon her.

Other abandonments occur when an inadequately assessed patient starts therapy, of whatever length, and turns out later to be unable to contain his violence, or suicidal fantasies, or to 'hear' interpretations. Often there is a hasty staff meeting – or even a supervision session! – where it is decided that the patient should end treatment when the therapist next goes on holiday, or some other convenient break. Some compensation for the patient is arranged, such as a day centre or stronger medication.

Effectively ditched, the patient is left feeling he has failed yet again. Proper Assessment could have prevented this. Once it has happened though, the treatment team must accept responsibility and the therapist be helped to explain the misappliance of dynamic therapy honestly, rather than leaving the burden of failure with the patient.

A very common form of abandonment is due to the rotation system for trainee psychiatrists, and the placement system for trainee clinical psychologists or counsellors. The patient must *always* be told from the outset the leaving date of the trainee, and patients should *always* be properly selected such that the depth and complexity of their treatment does not outstrip the trainee's capacity to give it. *Regular* quality clinical supervision *as opposed to line management* must *always* be on hand.

Any supervision of trainees must *always* include an invitation to them to explore their *feelings*, concerning both the patient and his material (counter-transference) and themselves as doubting, fearful, anxious trainees, without them having to worry that they are being evaluated for course or promotion purposes. Many trainees feel abandoned by their course leaders because this invitation is not made or they dare not accept it. They believe they must act more confident than they feel, to avoid being penalised.

Many courses might profitably explore the use of external supervisors. Granted, that before qualification the trainees have to be 'reported on' by supervisors, external or internal, but an external supervisor wears only one hat, enjoys more distance from the evaluative aspects of the course and is not party to the politics and interpersonal tensions that prevail in all training programmes. Furthermore, the supervisee's work to some extent reflects the supervisor's own, so she will want her supervisee to appear to be learning well. The supervisee knows she is unlikely to give an adverse opinion unless the circumstances really warrant it.

Back now, to the patient. Without proper Assessment, which among other things predicts the general course of the therapy's development, double abandonments occur. The first is when the patient is assigned (abandoned) to a therapist according to who happens to be available at the time and is left to stew. Should the patient then go through a specially bad patch and require hospitalisation, temporary hostel accommodation, a day support centre, a temporary increase or change in medication, no facilities are to hand and the only way to get the patient what he needs is to abandon him again, this time to another agency. Good Assessment would have meant such needs were anticipated and 'sleeping provision' laid on, to be 'woken up' at the very moment of need, the patient meanwhile confident that his therapist will continue to look after him the moment he is well enough to continue, or even support him through the crisis along with the extra provision.

Clinical cover is also essential for therapists' long holidays. Anticipating just what the need is likely to be and how to meet it is the job of Assessment. I am appalled at how often very vulnerable patients are left to cope alone for six or more weeks at a time. In supervision all supervisees must be helped to become aware of the impact of their absence and prepare patients properly for a break, not just inform them of the relevant dates.

If, in training new therapists, I were allowed to give only one ethical instruction, without a doubt it would be: 'Always do a thorough Assessment', thus ensuring that so far as is possible a patient gets the right length and type of therapy, any necessary adjuncts to therapy, a clear focus (Dynamic Formulation) to work on in therapy, and the right therapist in terms of experience, expertise, and temperament. I am thinking here of staff groups such as exist in student counselling services, mental health teams or outpatient psychiatric units. Different therapists possess not only different training and previous professional experience, but also different innate therapeutic gifts, as well as blind spots, which make them better with some patients than others. These strengths and weaknesses ought to be recognised and constructively exploited within a well-functioning team. All too often (to avert uncomfortable feelings of competitiveness?) they are denied and the patient is assigned on a strictly rotational 'fair' basis. With goodwill on both sides many patients and therapists can adjust to whatever partner they have been given, but it has to be said that some pairs will never work, while other therapies could be greatly speeded up given the right 'marriage'. The right temperamental fit can halve the time it takes to do a first-class Assessment, for instance.

Having paused to reiterate the centrality of Assessment in good therapy, I will continue with my 'dos' and 'don'ts' in the next chapter.

8 TEACHING PHILOSOPHY AND ETHICS THROUGH SUPERVISION (2)

DO ACKNOWLEDGE NEGATIVE FEELINGS TOWARD THE PATIENT

Feelings of goodwill and caring concern for the patient are taken for granted by the therapist/supervisee but need to be thought over occasionally, especially in the early stages of a training course. Such feelings are far from always induced by the lovable patient himself; rather are they the result of experiences, identifications and conflict resolutions in the therapist's own life. She has *developed* into a caring person and as such is able, generally speaking, to love even the most unlovable of personalities, for she understands that no one sets out to be unlovable – quite the reverse in fact – and that most objectionable behaviour, when properly analysed reveals a vulnerable human being seeking love and approval as much, if not more, than the rest of us.

However, there are some patients who, despite the therapist's open-mindedness, care and patience, do evoke very negative feelings in her. This causes much self-reproach in the therapist who is often too ashamed to bring up the matter in supervision, and certainly will not do so with a supervisor she is afraid of, intimidated by, does not know or does not trust. This point again clearly demonstrates the need for regular supervision with the same person, so that a relationship equivalent to the Therapeutic Alliance in therapy can be built up.

Negative feelings toward patients fall basically into two groups: those which are the result of the therapist's *transference to the patient*, which usually means that some aspect of the therapist's personality has not been sufficiently analysed in her own therapy and she is still 'at risk' with certain patients who 'spark off' that part of her; and those which Winnicott (1947) calls *objective coun-*

tertransference – natural responses to beastly behaviour, in other words.

Bringing about conscious recognition of negative feelings toward the patient, putting them in the right group and then helping the supervisee better manage them is an integral part of supervision. I am surprised at how often supervisees 'confess' to what they think are unprofessional feelings, or go on unconsciously denying them because of their quite unnecessary guilt.

It is not unethical to have bad feelings about a patient. It *is* unethical not to examine them.

In his seminal paper (*op. cit.*) Winnicott provides a list of circumstances that clearly show how the most normal of mothers hates her baby from the word go (as well as loving it). Hating of itself does not make her a bad mother: indeed it is the knowing about and containing of the hate in the infant's interest that makes her a good mother.

> Sentimentality is useless for parents, as it contains a denial of hate, and sentimentality in a mother is no good at all, from the infant's point of view.
>   It seems to me doubtful whether a human child as he develops is capable of tolerating the full extent of his own hate in a sentimental environment. *He needs hate to hate.* (My italics.)

With a particularly ill patient, be this temporary or long-standing, the therapist/supervisee has often to recognise that the patient is unable to acknowledge her efforts because he is unable to identify in any way at all with his therapist. Such a lack of recognition can easily engender hate; the therapist feels she is unwanted, unappreciated and has nothing to offer. Her unconscious hate often makes her remove him to hospital, have him drugged, or referred elsewhere. But if she is aware of this hate, then like the hating but reliable mother, she can refrain from retaliative attack and await better times.

Inexperienced and/or unconfident therapists sometimes need rewards from their patient that he does not have it in him to give, because of the very personality attributes that brought him into therapy. In Winnicott's words the hating therapist must contain his hate and 'seem to want to give, what is really only given because of the patient's needs'. Later on, as the patient improves, it becomes possible to tell him of and help him understand the therapist's former hate – though this is a most delicate matter of timing. Winnicott in the same paper says:

I believe an analysis is incomplete if even towards the end it
has not been possible for the analyst to tell the patient what he,
the analyst, did unbeknown for the patient whilst he was ill, in
the early stages. Until this interpretation is made the patient is
kept to some extent in the position of infant – one who cannot
understand what he owes to his mother.

I have worked with many supervisees who are parents, and who
seem relatively easily to tolerate hateful behaviour and attitudes of
their baby or adolescent offspring – though they grumble about it.
Yet working with patients this capacity seems to desert them; they
insist they have tried and tried but have become convinced they
cannot help a particular patient and he has got to go.

Although the supervision session is not for gossiping about family matters, I have found with regular supervisees that I pick up
bits of information about their domestic lives (sick children making
them late or forcing them to cancel etc.) and can weave these facts
into the supervision to show them how, if they can do it for their
own children, they must have the capacity to do it for patients.

DO NOT DENY A PATIENT'S WORLD VIEW
DIFFERENT FROM YOUR OWN

Despite personality differences, most sane, decent, intelligent human
beings share a *world view*. Without thinking about it much, they
assume that you ought to 'do as you would be done by', 'give and
take'; yet it is also important to stick up for yourself and your loved
ones. It is recognised too that 'you can't make an omelette without
breaking eggs' and 'the world is no rose garden'.

Most psychotherapy patients share this balanced philosophy
with their therapists so that everything the couple say to each
other is easily understood; the underlying value system is taken for
granted, needs no spelling out. Although she rarely thinks about it,
the therapist in fact cashes in on early family influences that, no
matter how pathological in other ways, enabled the patient see the
world in this reasonable light.

Sometimes though, a patient had no such help and has developed an idiosyncratic view of the world that differs markedly from
the therapist's, who can only be of help to him by finding out why
and how that view came about, and what internal problems such a
view continues to solve, despite the unhappy side-effects that
brought him to therapy.

Again, Assessment is vital. Consider two patients with identical symptoms of depression – early morning waking, poor appetite, physical slowing down, low self-esteem, excessive self-reproach, feelings of worthlessness and failure. The patient with the same world view as most of us may have temporarily lost faith in his balanced outlook but it will be restored once the underlying conflicts have been identified and resolved in therapy. In this case the depression has been the *result* of problems, not their cause. Relatively short-term therapy might well be indicated.

The other patient may be quite different despite the superficial similarities, and require a much longer treatment. All his life he has worn a depressive *lens*. Until the therapist looks at the world through this lens also, she will not understand him or feel she can be of help.

Her every intervention, *based on her own view of the world*, is greeted with a sigh: 'That may be right for others, but not for me. I'm just too awful/stupid/unimportant/undeserving.' No amount of reassurance, presenting contrary evidence, or attempts to fortify the Therapeutic Alliance changes the patient's self-perception. The therapist/supervisee either emotionally exhausts herself trying and failing to counteract the misery, becomes frustrated by the lack of progress and sees it as her failure to be a good therapist, or feels the patient is somehow in love with his depression and has no wish to let it go.

In supervision such reactions to the patient constitute vital clues. If an otherwise competent supervisee is feeling this way after several sessions there is a good chance that the treatment couple's failure to connect is because they are operating from different philosophical bases. Put another way, they have a different transference to the world as a whole, so they are not talking about the same entity when they discuss how the patient functions in it.

Case Example

Martha, a senior psychiatric social worker in her early thirties, saw Jane, my supervisee, for Assessment. Martha described herself as 'just a miserable person who should be put out of her misery like a dog'. Nonetheless, she was highly thought of in her career and had written many well-received papers. Her husband was utterly devoted to her. She explained that she had developed cunning tricks to get on with people, be popular at parties and with her husband's relatives, get along with suffering patients; but it was all phoney, a sort of game. All she really wanted was to curl up under the duvet and be miserable in peace. But she feared she might kill herself if she didn't keep up what she called her 'act'. Accordingly, she strictly rationed herself to only a few comforting 'temporary suicides' – lying alone in the dark thinking black thoughts – per week.

In supervision Jane said she truly felt for the patient's plight but she had to admit too, that she found Martha cold, cruel and arrogant. She felt her patient, though perfectly courteous, endured her every interpretation with disguised contempt. There was no real Alliance. Martha saw the work as a legalistic contract she was obliged to keep, just as she said life itself was something you were obligated to live and it was cheating to do the end bit – kill yourself rather than waiting to die – so as to get the whole farce over with.

I tried to get Jane to don her patient's lens, see the world as Martha saw it, and have a go at working out how such a bleak philosophy had developed.

All her young life Martha's mother had been in and out of hospital with a 'personality disorder' that erupted into fits of rage and serious emotional blackmail – suicide or abandonment threats, refusals to eat and so forth. She was especially invasive of her children's privacy, reading their diaries, going through their clothes. She regularly made scenes at school. She ridiculed any attempts they made to look attractive, scoffed at their games, and later their ambitions. Yet they were forced to admire, protect, humour and diplomatically 'manage' the mother, to avoid the stress of a usually public and humiliating admission to hospital by ambulance.

Martha's sister grew up to suffer intermittent schizophrenic episodes. One brother joined an enclosed order after a breakdown and another emigrated to New Zealand where he lived alone on a remote farm. Father stayed in the background and eventually left, so Martha hardly knew him. In her therapy sessions he was dismissed as a 'weak fool'.

Listening to the clinical material brought to supervision by Jane, I found Martha's most distressing symptom to be her unspoken conviction that she was incapable of love, which she rationalised by fixing to believe that love was but an illusion designed to help people imagine some point to life rather than recognise its true futility. This perspective on the world meant that life really did hold no meaning for her – it was just something to be got through. Such a cynical and self-destructive view was preferable to feeling that everyone in the whole world but her knew how to love and be loved. In spite of her misery she could tell herself the world was

*blind and only she saw it straight. This in turn led to some degree
of perverse self-esteem.*

*Even her husband, of whom she seemed fond and who was
constantly bombarded with her true depressive feelings as opposed
to the act she put on in public, was talked about in unloving
terms: 'He's so besotted he'll take anything and never complain.
Poor fool can't even see he's married an impostor.'*

*Jane tried hard, but could not grasp the idea of different 'world
views'. She could not accept that Martha's suicidal talk expressed a
real wish to die, that she truly believed love to be irrelevant.
'Everybody wants love, underneath', she insisted, 'that's what life
(i.e. my own world view!) is all about.'*

*Jane could not cope with the notion that a person may have to
be taught how to want love, shown that it is worth having. She
saw Martha's depression as a set of unpleasant signs and symptoms
which she could feel sorry about, but the patient herself as a rather
nasty type she simply did not like. She could not see Martha's
nihilism as an authentic belief system (with an unconscious protective purpose, as all belief systems have) at all. Neither of us felt
good about the supervision.*

*And then I dreamt about Jane's patient. On recounting my
dream Jane began to understand, and the therapy slowly improved.
Seeing the world through Martha's lifelong lens she developed real
compassion for her and tolerated the slowness of therapy much
better.*

*This was the dream. Martha's mother, a patrician Roman's
voluptuous wife (glossy ringlets, gold armbands and bare creamy
breasts) lolled on a couch eating grapes while a servant fanned her
with palm leaves. Martha, a babe bare but for her nappy, with
little Botticelli wings, arrived from nowhere, flying in reconnoitring
circles round the ceiling, in which direction pointed the full, lactat-
ing breasts. The circling became faster as a noise started up like
that of an angry hornet. Martha was closing in! Suddenly she
dived, suckled fast and hard on both nipples and darted away
again, cheeks bulging – there'd been no time to swallow – as the
mother's hand slapped furiously at the intrusion. Martha only just
escaped, hovered on the ceiling swallowing the milk as if it were
poison, but a poison that had to be taken to survive, before diving
again, having this time distracted her mother by throwing a choco-
late just beyond her reach. While she stretched out to claim it,
Martha pounced again.*

*Jane saw that Martha's world was a loveless place where to
survive you had to attack, steal, trick and deceive; where sur-*

vival and the eating of poison were synonymous; where there was no emotional loss because there had never been gain to start with. The experience of loss unites us as human beings; because of it we understand or try to understand one another. It creates an unspoken bond between most patients and their therapist. Haughty, superior, cold Martha had not learned about loss and could not bond because she had never been allowed to get and stay close in the first place. To withstand her mother's constant attacks and rejections she had had to become harder, colder and more loveless than her model.

Martha had read about loss in her social-work training of course, and could write fluently about it, but in therapy claimed she didn't really know what all the fuss was about!

Among her siblings Martha alone was able to hear and manage the mother, by rejecting any meaningful contact with her (even supposing it were on offer), and denying to herself that she had any needs at all for nurturance. I pointed out to Jane how her patient did this in the transference also, which was why she, Jane, was feeling so bad.

Jane began to see that she was trying to relate in the consulting room with an adult patient who had long since cut out the giving and receiving of love from her life altogether, but who as a result was left with a world where life was scarcely worth having. But look at her sister's and brothers' refusal to accept the non-existence of love, their hanging on to that useless mother. Had their eternal hope not driven them to madness and the living death of seclusion? Surely her capacity for 'acting normal' while secretly knowing the rest of the world was deluded, put her in a better position than them?

Therapy has to be long term in a case like this. There are no short cuts and it is unethical to attempt any. Therapy would aim at helping Martha to trace the development of her own world view and perhaps she would eventually elect to modify it. But in the end it would not be just intellectual knowledge about herself that would alter Martha's philosophy, but a long, corrective experience with her therapist that would give her the chance to taste something of what she missed as an infant. She must learn how to love, and the value of love, from the very beginning, from babyhood, and from a 'mother' who will not repeat the original emotional coldness, as Jane, her therapist, was at first threatening to do.

Jane had complained, accurately, that no Alliance existed. By the time this kind of patient is able to make an Alliance she will be getting ready to leave.

DO HONOUR RELIGIOUS AND CULTURAL DIFFERENCES

We all know how important it is to respect others' religious and cultural beliefs, but in practice it is much easier to honour them in the letter than the spirit. In psychotherapy lip-service and common courtesy are not enough. If they are to maintain authentic dialogue, patients and therapists sometimes have to agree to disagree over some moral or social precept. Sometimes a real struggle with the other person's culture or religion has to be admitted. Much debate and mutual education may have to occur before any worthwhile therapeutic work can be achieved.

Case Example

Miriam, aged 29, a member of my private therapeutic group, came from a tightly-knit Jewish family. One half of the 'tribe', as she called it, lived in Israel, the other in London. Everyone in the group was happy about her taking time off to attend funerals and feast days, when the whole family came together in Israel for the necessary rituals, which everyone was fascinated to hear about on her return.

Miriam's problems with the group started when she burst into tears one night, saying she was fed up of hearing about other people's partners. She had never had a serious boyfriend, and while she was no oil painting she couldn't be that ugly, surely? Everyone realised she had been left out in this regard and the whole group now guiltily focussed its attention upon her.

Miriam explained how all the suitors her parents brought home failed to stir her in the slightest. Some she had dated for a while to keep the parents happy, but eventually she tired of them. All group members accepted the fact that courtships were 'arranged' in this way in Miriam's community, but found it hard to cope with the implications of that fact. Miriam had both Jewish and non-Jewish friends at work and the college where she did an evening course, and the group encouraged her to develop a yet wider circle in the hope of meeting Mr Right. She explained that she just could not take a non-Jewish man home. It would distress her family too much.

One group member argued that if you leave choice of partner to your parents what can you expect but someone dead boring and respectable? Another brave member said to be honest she thought

Miriam was hiding behind her religion and was just frightened to go and get her own man. Again Miriam insisted her Jewishness prevented her from doing socially what non-Jewish people did; she was at the mercy of her parents.

I was rather silent throughout the debate that followed. I had always felt that Miriam had some difficulties in the area of sexual maturation and could see how her Jewishness protected her from determining her own future in this regard. But as I watched her, pleading on the edge of tears that they didn't understand what 'family' meant to Jews, I realised too that she was right. Everyone in this room bar her was passionately committed to individualism; in the last analysis the integrity of the Self was what counted. For Miriam it was the integrity of the family.

'You would give up a man you really loved if they could not accept him?' the group asked incredulously. 'If I had to, yes. But my heart would break all the same. I can love as strongly as any of you. My parents aren't monsters. They love me and what my happiness as I want theirs. I can't hurt them. It's not right.'

This group found it very hard both to respect Miriam's Jewish background and at the same time insist she work on separation from her family, now she was an adult. Such a concept of adulthood did not sit easily with her.

There are no easy answers to this kind of dilemma, but it is important that 'political correctness' does not prevent people in a therapeutic environment from talking honestly about culture clashes.

In another group, a young man who had been sexually abused by his mother was applying to train for the Catholic priesthood. I sensed that several group members doubted this was his true vocation, saw enforced celibacy as a way of getting round his problems of sexual identity, but were afraid to say much about it for fear of seeming to challenge the sincerity of his faith. After weeks of 'atmosphere' each time he spoke of his application, it was I, as the group conductor, who had to bring the whole topic into the light.

Exercising tact, respect and caution over matters of religion and culture should not be the same as maintaining a taboo about them.

I once made the inexcusable error of asking a new Muslim patient his *Christian* name. I shall never forget the look on his face when he told me what happened to anyone in his war-torn community purporting to be Christian. I apologised and asked if we could start again. Eventually I was pardoned and the therapy went well. It is amazing how much can be forgiven, if the patient senses genuine goodwill.

DO (FOR HEAVEN'S SAKE) LAUGH!

I am not proposing here that patients and therapists squander their 50 minutes by recounting endless yarns about Englishmen, Irishmen and Scotsmen, but I am saying that humour has a vital place in therapy. Patient and therapist should be able to laugh at themselves in the presence of the other. They should be able to tease each other: I cannot remember how many patients have given me juicy material and then tilted their head just as I do and said: 'Now, I know what Auntie Wyn would say ...' followed by an interpretation mimicking my own intonation and vocabulary.

Jokes, puns and humorous analogies can be made about the material that save long minutes of elaboration and interpretation. Therapy is a serious business but it doesn't have to be an earnest one.

Humour is a form of play, metaphorical communication: therapy without play is dead therapy. For a cogent and creative extension of this idea, see Jean Collard's (1995) unpublished dissertation: 'Some functions of metaphor in the therapeutic setting'.

True, there is also defensive humour – sarcastic wit (on either side) disguising envy; manic flight denying internal despair or the effects of external tragedy; joint laughter at others' expense that mocks and undermines; humour thinly masking sexism, ageism, homophobia and so on. A skilled therapist or supervisor understands the uses and abuses of humour and acts accordingly. She is well aware that inappropriate laughter is material for analysis, not collusion.

In supervision the supervisee often obtains vast relief from tension, anxiety and a crippling sense of responsibility concerning a very worrying or wearing patient, through what on the face of it seems like a callous or frivolous joke, hooted at by supervisor and supervisee alike. While joining in, the supervisor notes the degree of stress under which the supervisee labours and makes a mental note to comment at an appropriate time.

Case Example

Eddie's therapy was into its fourth year. His childhood was filled with loss – both parents, grandparents and later a sister. He had worked hard on these matters and understood the source and development of his personality problems very well. All that remained was the grieving, which for a year he had been unable to do, though he recognised that the permanent lump in his throat and ever threatening panic attacks were his system sending his body messages to get on with it.

For months therapy was in the doldrums. We grew bored and dispirited together. Then one day, occasioned by an item on the morning news, the grieving came. Eddie sobbed and beat the couch, his frame heaving with the effort. I was greatly moved but held my peace and waited.

As the crying became more controlled and regular, I found it was time to end the session. 'I'm afraid we have to stop for today', I said. Eddie took a huge breath, swung his legs up in the air and over the side of the couch. Seated on its edge he clapped his hands and rubbed them together. His face still wet with tears he said loudly: 'Amazing how time flies when you are enjoying yourself.'

We both laughed. But we looked at each other as Eddie left and I am certain we understood each other. He hated me for ending the session after we had waited so long for this catharsis. But he knew I had to keep the boundaries intact if this were to be a safe enough place for him to express the years of repressed pain and yet still manage to run his life without a complete breakdown. We both knew too, that his remark was another example of the manic defence mechanism he had used all his life, but were agreed that on this occasion it was being deployed consciously and appropriately. After all, he would be running his factory in 20 minutes and I had another patient in 10. That humorous reaction had been as much for my sake as his own and I knew he saw my look of gratitude behind the laughter. After four years there was no need for either of us to speak these things. The shared humour said it all.

Case Example 2

Humorous acceptance, rather than puritanical adherence to interpretive technique can often benefit the patient. I once had an elderly lady in treatment who I felt was better but who seemed reluctant to terminate. One day, feeling relaxed, the sun streaming in through the window and birds singing in the garden, she fell into a doze. To my horror she started to slip inch by inch to the edge of the couch and I was certain she was about to fall off. I wished to prevent this without waking her, but could scarcely *manhandle her sleeping body for fear of what such an act might mean to her. In the end I talked softly to her, telling her to move her leg a bit to the right, left arm up, right arm down etc. She received these instructions without opening her eyes and when safely positioned began to contentedly snore.*

I spent the rest of the session smiling to myself. She derived more benefit from her watched-over sleep than from any interpretation I might have been able to make in her waking state. Being watched over as a child was utterly foreign to her, though she always longed for it despite having come to terms with its absence in therapy. Soon after this incident she was able to start discussing termination.

Humour in psychotherapy is a large, important and much neglected topic. A comprehensive review of the literature can be found in Mahrer and Gervaize (1984). It is important to maintain a balanced view of the pros and cons of letting humour enter the session and not be led by fashions and fads. To this end I shall close this chapter with two opposing quotes, in my view equally valid.

Kubie (1991), writing in psychoanalytic vein, argues that humour can be damaging in the following ways:

1. Therapist use of humour may block or arrest free association.

2. Therapist use of humour may confuse the client by creating unnecessary concerns as to whether the therapist is serious or not.

3. Therapist use of humour may cause the client to accept that which *is* serious as being less serious than it actually is.

4. Client use of humour may increase ego defence and thus extend the period of therapy unnecessarily.

5. Client use of humour masks pain and thus makes therapy more, rather than less, difficult.

6. Excessive use of therapist humour may unduly restrict the client's expression of fear, anger, remorse or pain – he or she may not wish to spoil the therapist's 'fun'.

7. Humour makes the therapist more visible than he or she ought to be, since it impairs 'necessary incognito'.

In a fascinating paper, Mann (1991), an art therapist, while agreeing the dangers of too free a use of humour, nonetheless sums up:

> Humour in common with other feelings is part of a healthy relationship, and the therapeutic one is no exception. It is surely the possession of such feelings that makes the therapy alive between two human begins. Humour should no more be expelled from therapy than should any other emotion; though excessive humour from the therapist should be guarded against. Humour may allow the therapist and patient to share an acknowledged feeling in a manner that does not burden the patient with the therapist's personal life. In this respect humour is far less destructive than if the therapist openly expressed rage or envy.

He concludes:

> Humour will not make our work less serious, but may, if used appropriately, enable patients to develop the capacity for a richer experience of themselves and others and enhance their capacity to play and have a complete human experience.

Hear! Hear!

9 CLINICAL TEACHING IN
SUPERVISION (1)

The teaching of good clinical practice and ethical awareness go
hand in hand and can only be separated for illustrative purposes,
as I here attempt to do. Therefore to a considerable extent this
chapter and the next will reflect the preceding two, despite the
fresh perspective.

All efforts to make sense of the session material, in and out of
supervision, and any subsequent discussion of conclusions reached
with the patient, must be tempered with an acute awareness of
whether and how, to what extent and when, the patient can make
use of any understanding reached to further his healing. A realisation of what the material *means*, even when there is corroborative
evidence, does not automatically justify its unprocessed relay to the
patient: there must be great consideration of its likely effect. It
should be remembered also, that withholding understanding
through fear, uncertainty or lack of confidence can also have harm-
ful consequences.

The therapist's prime responsibility is not to decode the patient's
productions, 'correct' them and send them straight back to him, but
to support and develop the healing process by whatever means are
most appropriate at the time. This often requires the storing of some
or all understanding and the making of many tentative formulations
until the patient is ready to hear or at least consult over them.
Uncertain supervisees, especially when still in training, tend to be so
relieved to have understood a piece of material they cannot wait to
display their knowledge to the patient as proof of their therapeutic
competence. They need to learn self-restraint.

In these two chapters I shall consider the commonest clinical
problems that in my own experience have arisen – and still do – in
supervision. They can be grouped together under five headings.
First there are specific queries of which the supervisee is con-

sciously aware and with which she requests direct help from the supervisor. Second, there are problems and issues of which the supervisee is not aware, but which the supervisor spots as she listens to the supervisee's account of the work in hand. Third, are those that neither party has spotted but which make themselves apparent through the interpersonal process in the supervision session itself. Fourth, are 'in between' difficulties. Both supervisee and supervisor know roughly where the clinical problem lies but can't put their finger on it until they have together teased out and ordered the material much further. This involves the supervisee not learning *what* to think, but *how* to think. Fifth come problems of technique; the supervisee may know what needs doing but not actually how to carry it out.

1. SPECIFIC ISSUES BROUGHT BY SUPERVISEE

These are many and varied, but broadly speaking can be classified under (a) the Dynamic Formulation (though the supervisee may not call it that), (b) some aspect of the transference, and (c) the apparent impossibility of short-term therapy.

(a) The Dynamic Formulation

The supervisee's complaint is usually: 'Despite several sessions I just can't get the hang somehow', or 'There doesn't seem to be a focus. The patient talks freely enough. I have loads of information, but there's no pattern.' Most frequently of all, I hear: 'I'm useless with this person. We are just going round in circles.'

In my previous book (Bramley 1996) I examined the whole business of how to make the Dynamic Formulation during Assessment so will not repeat that here. The point that does need making here is how often supervisees fail to see what is under their nose, expecting that they must produce lengthy, complex, 'deep' formulations that reveal their (the supervisee's) extraordinary vision.

A very anxious supervisee brought her patient, Jonathon, complaining that after three sessions of Assessment she was no nearer making a Dynamic Formulation. I asked her to tell me what she knew about him and how he presented himself. I then quickly arrived at the following Formulation: 'However much this man behaves to the contrary, deep down he believes he does not matter, because he has ample evidence that he did not matter to his parents. All his relation-ship break-ups and off-putting attitudes stem from that.'

The supervisee was astounded. 'Well that much is obvious. I knew that', she said, disgusted and disappointed I hadn't come up with anything more profound.

What she failed to appreciate was just how deeply ingrained this unconscious self-precept ('I am a person who does not matter') was. Jonathon could not make normal emotional demands in any relationship, nor fight to keep relationships he prized. Women found him superior, bored, distant and apparently disinterested in them. In truth, far from being self-sufficient and confident, he was totally unable to cope with intimacy. His defensive behaviour was always interpreted as coldness and loftiness so he fulfilled his own prophecy by driving friends and partners away.

Therapy for Jonathon should consist in the repeated interpretation of these defences, as they happened in the current professional and personal relationships he reported, and very importantly in his deal-ings with the therapist herself (who disliked what she called his 'snootiness' and who, like everyone else, found him distant and cool). In treatment she needed to assist him to trace the development of these defences against 'not mattering', and show him implicitly, by the way she dealt with him, that he did indeed matter to her and she was not fooled by the mask of ennui he wore; she could see through to his pain.

The problem was, that due to the lack of a proper Dynamic Formulation, the supervisee had not seen through to his pain. Nei-ther had she realised that her work lay in making conscious for him his own appalling sense of insignificance, so he could at last begin to challenge it.

To me the therapeutic road seemed clear, but the therapist/supervisee had seen in the material only one more bit of parental deprivation; we therapists are hearing that stuff all the time. She failed to recognise that on this occasion the patient's negative self-image resulting from it, and his extreme defences against facing it, were at the very core of his problems.

A simple formulation does not necessarily mean a superficial one!

Another example follows of a supervisee unable to accept the depths to which a simple Dynamic Formulation can reach:

This supervisee brought June, an intelligent, well-read woman in her thirties, who had witnessed multiple violent happenings, implied and actual, in her family, which contrasted with her parents' insistence

throughout her life that theirs was a loving, supportive household,
highly respected, much admired and envied by all in the neighbour-
hood. By circuitous routes June discovered a feisty grandma who ran
off with a Jamaican and got pregnant; a couple of seriously criminal
cousins; the fact that her mother and aunt were both sexually abused
by a family member and a never explained 'cot death'. She herself
had had very disturbing nightmares throughout her childhood, which
no one, not even the family doctor would discuss with her. She had
often feared she was mad, but sensed she must never 'let on'.

   The supervisee was puzzled and dissatisfied with the treatment
because June had read all the psychology books and seemed to
know all the answers. She knew she had to bring all the family
secrets into the open, challenge the lies and half-truths told inside
the family, allow herself to be angry at the mental confusion in
which she was forced to live as a child. As she aired each and
every secret, lie, example of double-dealing, she seemed glad that
the supervisee was 'with' her, trying to understand what it must
have been like for her. The supervisee however, felt she was con-
tributing very little because the patient understood her childhood
situation all too well.

   'Why does she keep coming?' asked the bewildered supervisee. 'I
am not doing anything for her.' I asked if there was anything
unusual or striking in the way June offered her material and the
supervisee said, well, only that she had this preoccupation with
minute detail. Every incident from the past was gone over with a
fine-tooth comb. When the supervisee commented that such an
incident must have felt lonely, or scary, must have struck her
younger self this way or that, June would listen attentively, then
reply with great seriousness and concentration: 'Well it almost *felt*
like that, but it was just a bit more this way, or that way.' June
had to feel that her therapist understood and accepted every nu-
ance of her childhood experience as if she had been there. *This*
fastidiousness over getting it right became almost boring for the
supervisee, who felt she wasn't progressing at all with this patient.

   I commented that it sounded as if the patient were sifting evi-
dence, like a pathologist; or going through years of accounts like an
auditor. We then both came to the realisation at once that what
June was seeking in therapy was a Witness, someone to verify her
experience, check out and legitimise all the evidence she needed to
bring. The transference, if it could be described thus, was to the
whole therapeutic situation. The consulting room was a court of
law. On trial was June's family and she was chief prosecutor. The
supervisee was helping her to organise her case, lending another

pair of eyes and ears where the patient, because of early confusing experiences, could not trust her own.

It was essential for the patient's healing to know that justice had at last been seen (by the therapist) to be done. The traumas could be put away and she could move on from her troubled past to a future where she might have more confidence in her own perceptions and judgments. The therapist's task was to stand Witness while June put her 'haunted house' in order. It was as simple, yet as vitally important as that!

Yet whenever afterwards I followed up June's case, which seemed to me to be progressing well, the supervisee would say gloomily: 'Oh she's all right I suppose, but I'm still only the blooming witness. I'd rather have a proper job to do.'

The supervisee could not see that she was a Witness in the archetypal, not merely the legal, sense. Like the Lone Ranger, or some other archetypal cowboy, she was to ride into town (the consulting room), stand witness to the trials and tribulations of the local inhabitants (the patient), commit herself to Right against Might (June's family), indulge in some troubleshooting (therapy) to restore power and authority to its rightful owner (June), before riding off into the sunset. She found this role hard to value, seeing it as less important than standing in for a particular person – the patient's mother, sisters, or aunts. She wanted to represent a person, even a bad one, rather than a thing, a quality, a function. She felt she wasn't doing real therapy.

But 'real therapy' is what the patient needs (and will often show or tell the therapist she needs), not what clever tricks the therapist longs to perform.

(b) The Transference

Recognising the transference is one thing; interpreting it in a way that is helpful to the patient can be quite another. Sometimes quite exceptional sensitivity and tact are called for, and inexperienced supervisees need help to develop this. Likely transferences should be predicted and discussed at Assessment so that therapists are not placed in unnecessary danger, or patients unnecessarily provoked. This is why supervisors should be available at the very start of treatment and not just called in when there are problems.

A fellow supervisor told me of one of her supervisees who had started coming for supervision after seeing the patient under discus-

sion, Dick, for nearly two years. The supervisee worked alone at home, in private practice. The late involvement meant my colleague had had no say over selection or Assessment of the patient, which she was very much to regret.

Dick had been diagnosed as: 'Personality disorder with mood swings' by the assessing psychiatrist who had referred him to the supervisee for private help. There was a history of temper tantrums as a child and black, angry moods as an adult with occasional bouts of hitting the furniture; but, to the psychiatrist's knowledge, he had never hit a person.

The supervisee doubted the diagnosis and herself judged Dick to be suffering problems based around inability to separate from significant figures, which always resulted in the aforementioned black moods and some violence. He'd had much separation foisted on him in his life, but the supervisee felt the most traumatic to have been at the age of four, when his widowed mother (who he felt neglected him in favour of her job and boyfriend) decided to move house without consulting him at all. They would live nearer the boyfriend. Even more importantly, the gran who had looked after him since birth, and who lived just down the street, would no longer have charge of him in the daytime: a nurse was to be hired. He was a shy boy who found it very hard to make new contacts and now he would also be separated from the only two chums he had, and to whom he was devoted. He never forgave his mother.

The supervisee got on well with Dick and felt that in the transference she was mostly the beloved gran. However, around the time the supervisee came to see my colleague, the supervisee's husband bought a new house to be near his work and to be able to provide better facilities for social/business activities now he was promoted. The sale had gone through very suddenly and the supervisee could only give Dick a few weeks notice of the change. She reassured him that there was to be a consulting room in the new house and he could still come and see her.

Dick was furious, missed several sessions, then returned to say he was going to leave. If he stayed he would beat her up. Didn't she know what she was doing? Of course she did, it was just that clearly she didn't care. Suddenly the supervisee had become the mother who treated him so badly as a child. He seemed to the supervisee to be actually reliving the history, not just remembering it. The supervisor wondered about diagnosis and whether in fact the patient was on the border of psychosis.

The threats continued. The supervisee took the line she had been taught on her course, which was to negotiate a contract *whereby she would hear out all his rage but if there was any physical violence she would not go on seeing him. Quite properly she arranged for someone to be in the house during this patient's session. And lastly she persisted with her interpretation of the transference; that Dick was seeing her as if she were his mother.*

Dick's rage was barely controllable. He refused to attend sessions at the new house. He yelled at the supervisee that like his mother she had never consulted him; the deal was struck behind his back and then she gave the minimum notice possible. In fact he had seen the house up for sale in the estate agent's window and told himself it was some kind of mistake; his therapist would never do that to him, not with her knowing all she did about his past.

This case raises questions about diagnosis, referral, Assessment and the desirability of working alone in a building with 'personality disorders' of the potentially violent sort. But from the point of view of transference, it highlights the need not only to state what the transference is, and how it is operating, but to show the patient that the therapist knows how he feels as a victim of that transference. The supervisee, like many, was hanging on for dear life to what she had been taught. She mistakenly believed that transference interpretation of itself, if repeated often enough, would magically calm the patient down.

My own feeling is that showing Dick that she could imagine the full force of his feelings (their resulting from transference didn't make them one whit less real or hurtful) might have been better than reiterating 'you are reacting to me as if I were your bad mother', which served only to make the young man even angrier. In addition, she might have steered him toward the misery and loneliness beneath the rage now, as then, and got him to cry, thus defusing the urge to hit out.

It's easy for me to talk of course. It wasn't me in that very frightening position. But it is essential that we supervisors help our supervisees not just to identify and announce what any transference might be, but also to use their imagination and emotion, to put themselves in the transference-gripped shoes of the patient so as to deal sufficiently sensitively with him.

(c) Short-term Work

Alas, the current financial and political climate dictates that many patients in the public sector – and increasingly patients scraping together a bit of cash for private treatment too – can only be offered very limited therapeutic opportunities. In GP practices and colleges especially, as little as four or five sessions are often the norm. Such absurd policies need to be fought, but in the meantime improved, efficient Assessment techniques need to be taught on training courses and enhanced in supervision, such that those patients who can benefit from short-term work are sifted from those for whom short-term treatment could be worse than no treatment at all.

Supervisees have to be helped to accept the reality and frustrations of short-term work. A gallon of therapy cannot be squeezed into a pint pot. The object of short-term therapy can seldom be cure, or even a thorough examination of all the patient's history.

Usually, in the first session, the patient will give an account of 'where it hurts', in other words the issues that are hottest for him at the moment. It is the therapist's job to try to provide him with some appreciation of the dynamics causing the pain and ideally, though it is not always possible, some clue as to their origins. She can sometimes highlight also how the same dynamic features disturb other areas of his life and relationships. At the very least he ends up knowing what is psychologically happening inside him when the symptoms strike. He has made a start on his difficulties.

Mr Jones is having awful conflict with his boss, who on calm reflection he can see is not that bad: 'He just gets up my nose with his nit-picking demands and always checking up on me, waiting for me to do something wrong ...'

The therapist asks if he experiences this kind of problem elsewhere. (The GP has told her Mr Jones' blood pressure is up and he's taking time off work for 'stress' so there's no doubt the conflict at work must be quite serious.) He ponders awhile and recalls the rows with his father-in-law before he died; an office cricket team he once walked out of because of ugly spats with the captain; and oh yes, his ex-bank manager, a cocky little sod. He goes on to tell the therapist how he has trained his own son to stand up for himself, not to take any nonsense from the other kids or teachers.

The therapist begins to feel that Mr Jones may have been bullied as a child and asks him about this. He says he liked school, and got on well with everybody, though he was a bit shy: 'All fingers and thumbs, you know, awkward.'

'Father?' probes the therapist. He turns out to have been asthmatic and very much in the background. But the topic of family has drawn the interest of the patient, who starts to talk about an older brother he never got on well with, 'a sneery type who once stepped on my glasses just for fun'.

As the session progresses, evidence mounting to support this hunch, the therapist encourages Mr Jones to talk more about memories of childhood; helps him to look back with her, from the perspective of adulthood, at how, as a child, he was placed in his family – the close attachment to his mum, her pleasure at his excellent school reports, and the subsequent rivalry (which till now he had not realised) experienced by his brother, leading to vengeful behaviour.

She comments that beneath his fear of his older brother, much rage must have lurked. Now that he was big and strong and others looked up to him, he could at last afford to stand up to the brother in the shape of these transference figures; but in so doing was only shooting himself in the foot, for in actuality these people, difficult though they might be, did not carry the murderous feelings towards him that his brother had.

Presented with what amounts to the Dynamic Formulation, Mr Jones starts looking at how to get these feelings under control, now he understands their origin.

This is a tidy piece of very brief therapy with a good outcome, providing the therapist accepts from the start that there can be no fuller explorations – say of his relations with wife and mother, of his entire rather than localised approach to aggression, or of any other 'stress' factors leading to his physical problems. A narrow focus and a willing patient can produce tangible, if limited results, if the therapist is prepared to shrink her usual therapeutic horizons.

But what about the *patient's* expectations? Without overly discouraging him, he needs to be told the truth. Miracles cannot be expected to happen in four meetings. But some kind of attempt may be made to help him to 'get a handle' on his problem, see it in a fresh light, so that he can go home and work on himself by himself.

Where problems and symptoms are diffuse and no immediate focus can be found, the supervisee must be helped to send the patient back to the GP or other referral agent with a confident recommendation that he receive longer-term help from a more appropriate source – another private practitioner with specialised experience, or hospital outpatient unit; or where formal therapy is thought not to be suitable, perhaps a day centre in combination with some supportive help from the local mental health team. There is no shame in admitting that she herself has not been able to cure the patient. What she *has* hopefully accomplished is a competent Assessment to determine what sort of approach would be most profitable for him.

Short-term work can turn out to be the treatment itself, albeit a treatment with limited aims; it can be an Assessment, leading to a

firm decision not to do any further treatment; or it can be an intro-
duction to and preparation for treatment elsewhere. Often a very
anxious or depressed person can be helped to see the outline of what
till now has seemed an amorphous mass of misery, and accordingly
given hope and containment. The therapist, still half in the dark
herself due to shortage of time, may share some clues she has found
with the patient, for him to be going on with, while awaiting further
treatment which this therapist is not in this setting permitted to
provide, but which she will recommend to the referrer.

Supervision should aim to discourage the belief so prevalent in
supervisees that if only they were sufficiently clinically adept, all
patients could be helped by short-term therapy. They should be
assisted to see the value of Assessment and advice to the referrer, and
in preparation of the patient for further treatment. They should be
actively dissuaded from regarding these as second-class solutions, and
themselves as second-class therapists for carrying them out.

Last but by no means least, they should be encouraged to advise,
protest to, and educate 'those upstairs', when unrealistic clinical provision makes their work impossible. Protecting their work by insisting on the right tools for the job protects patients and preserves their
right to adequate treatment.

2. PROBLEMS SPOTTED BY THE SUPERVISOR

These can generally be housed under three roofs. First, all dynamic
therapy necessitates the deployment of thinking, feeling and intuition by the therapist, and different practitioners are more comfortable with one mode than another. There is bound to be natural
variation in supervisees, but any extreme imbalance among the
three modalities should be noticed and redressed by the supervisor.

Second, I have noted among supervisees an alarmingly widespread misunderstanding – and often downright ignorance – of the
significant differences between the practice of psychoanalysis and
the practice of broad spectrum psychotherapy. Vast numbers of
needless supervision problems arise from this confusion.

Third, there are those problems which the supervisee believes
concern the clinical material, which she is failing to comprehend
and manage, but which the supervisor comes to realise are problems that should have been prevented much earlier. These are
problems to do with an unsatisfactory referral or a faulty treatment
setting, rather than the patient's productions.

(a) An imbalance in thinking, feeling and intuition

Some supervisees have a prodigious memory and a mathematical flair that ensures they rapidly absorb and sort data, weighing up probabilities and constructing hypotheses that the rest of us take twice as long to reach and by a much more laborious route. Married with psychological intuition – that hard-to-define ability to process evidence before it has properly manifested itself in the session, that 'second sight' therapists must innately possess, however embryonically, and which they develop and hone with experience – such a supervisee possesses powerful tools indeed. However, she must be helped to restrain this force sometimes, and instead attend to whatever capacity she has for empathy; so that the patient, once having felt understood, identified with, is in better shape to take on board the supervisee's intellectual observations.

Similarly, the supervisee who has experienced much suffering in her life or had to endure the suffering of close relatives for years on end, may be tempted to overdo the empathy, without of course realising it, because she is so skilled at it and derives esteem-maintaining feedback from the patient who is amazed to find how thoroughly his till now isolating pain is appreciated, almost shared. Such appreciation, while an essential component in therapy, especially in the maintaining of the Therapeutic Alliance, is of little use on its own. The patient must also be helped to theory-build about his psychological state, its origins in the past and its current re-enactments, and be assisted to tackle these in the transference to the therapist and in his relations outside the consulting room.

Constant emoting on the part of the supervisee/therapist occupies all her mental space, squeezing out that empty area which should be vigilantly guarded at all times, so that intuitive ideas, thoughts, feelings and connections can jump into it. To allow intuition to operate untrammelled, the supervisee must learn how to *distance* herself emotionally from her patient, while remaining available to him. No mean feat! If there is too much investment in 'getting alongside him' as the jargon has it, necessary distance becomes impossible.

The right therapeutic stance is one of looking at the session through a telescope – both ends at once! On hearing this kind of advice supervisees often feel their supervisor is getting old and jaundiced: how can cutting off from the patient ever be justified? I would rather turn it the other way round and ask: how can total absorption in the patient's pain be right, however much both parties enjoy it, when a floating area of non-prejudicial *attention*

(Coltart 1993), a state of suspended awareness, readiness without anxiety, an emptying of the mind's and heart's contents while retaining their highly-tuned receptors, is central and irreplaceable for the psychodynamic understanding of any patient and the understanding of the therapist/supervisee's own reaction to that patient?

Half of the therapeutic practitioner should be in the chair, empathising with the patient, the other half standing behind that chair, dispassionately *thinking*, while managing the overall therapeutic situation. This management function includes maintaining a space in her mind where intuitive activities can take place.

The supervisor needs to be aware of the supervisee's strengths and weaknesses in this triple area of thinking, feeling and intuition; must help her see that to offer theories and models before the patient has had a chance to ventilate his feelings and have them understood, is as unhelpful as empathising at the expense of any attempt to grapple with the meaning of the pain being expressed. Intuitive knowledge can be very exciting, but the supervisee must be taught to hold on to intuitions when the patient is too engaged in catharsis to hear them, or is associating comfortably in a direction that, if the therapist is patient enough, will get him to the same insight himself – much more esteem-building for him than having to be told.

Every supervisor too, has a unique combination of thinking, feeling and intuitive chemistry in her make-up. It is important that supervisees are not too equally matched with their supervisor in this regard. If, for instance, supervisee and supervisor both excel in empathy and are somewhat short on intuition or data processing, they may end up with a mutual admiration society but not much learning for the supervisee.

Providing the gulf is not too wide, making the couple distrusting or even hostile to one another, I believe it's a good idea to have a supervisee and supervisor partnership where there is considerable difference in temperament, despite some common ground. A thinker and a feeler for example, have much to teach each other, for as surely as patients teach their therapists, so too do supervisees train their supervisors.

(b) Lack of appreciation of the differences between Psychoanalysis and Broad Spectrum Psychotherapy

Many supervisees say wistfully in supervision that they would feel more in control of the therapy they are reporting if only they could ask the patient a few direct questions, or interrupt him occasionally, or move him into a different subject area. But they feel inhibited from so doing by their training, which has erroneously led them to believe they should act at all times like the classical analyst, never treating the patient's flow of associations as anything less than sacred. Neither should they themselves speak unless they are certain that what they are about to utter is both complete and accurate.

Small wonder they have problems. Therapists who have to take on all-comers, be this in the public sector or their private practice, absolutely must do an Assessment to see whether and how this patient might be treated and by whom. Analysts as a rule have patients sent to them who have already been Assessed by a qualified therapeutic consultant who has judged them suitable for analysis, so can straight away afford to opt for classical free associative techniques and wait patiently (for years of treatment lie ahead) for the various problem areas to emerge in their own time and way.

An Assessment demands the (subtle) eliciting of a factual and psychological history, a record of the patient's key relationships and their workings at different stages of his development, an active seeking for current emotional conflicts that link with previous ones, and thus the attachment of meaning, however hazy at first, to presenting symptoms. None of this can be achieved in the short space of time (compared with analysis) allocated to broad spectrum work, without some considerable *conversation* taking place, rather than endless patient monologue, much of which will be padding and waffle, the new nervous patient sensibly protecting himself from revealing too much till he trusts his therapist, which he will have little chance to do if she adopts the sphinx-like features of the 'incognito' analyst!

The problem appears to be that many training courses, keen to be seen as accreditable, respectable, properly psychodynamic in their approach, have equipped their trainees only to practise watered-down psychoanalysis. Their graduates have not been alerted to the quite different and broader demands of general psychotherapeutic practice and so feel constrained and self-doubting when faced with the need to perform an Assessment they have not been trained how to do. As a supervisor I frequently find that neither have they realised that such a procedure might be necessary at all! If a GP, general psychiatrist, non-therapeutically trained priest, voluntary welfare worker or even a friend thinks this patient needs therapy, that is good enough for them: flattered, they proceed to try to provide it, irrespective of any institutional, time, or training constraints under which they will have to labour, let alone the clinical state of the patient.

For a much fuller examination of doing therapy by 'conversational' means, see *Forms of Feeling* (Hobson 1985), and for an actual case-study see Michael Barkham's and Robert Hobson's paper (1989): 'Exploratory therapy in two-plus-one sessions'.

Every patient will fit somewhere along a continuum that has at one end 'suitability for classical analysis' (in this context a treatment largely based on witnessed monologue), and at the other end 'suitability for short-term dynamic work' (in this context a treatment based on conversation). It is only along a short middle section of this continuum that the techniques of psychoanalysis and dynamic psychotherapy can be said to blur: it matters not which kind of therapist – psychoanalytic or broad spectrum dynamic – this patient sees, providing the therapist possesses the necessary expertise. What I would claim very strongly however, is that to place any patient accurately along that continuum and thus locate the right therapist, an Assessment is imperative, conducted either by the (broad spectrum) treating therapist herself, who can then tailor her subsequent therapy to patient need; or by a qualified (and I stress *qualified*) Assessor, who will then refer on to an appropriately equipped practitioner.

In broad spectrum work the therapist must often operate, at least initially, in ways with which the analyst is unfamiliar. Before starting, or between doing dynamic work, she may have to manage a crisis, or sit out a period when an ill patient is taking strong medication and analysis, even if appropriate, would not get through the fog. Because of the shortage of time, she is obliged – unlike the analyst – to offer possible interpretations before they are anything like crystallised: often patient and therapist have together to struggle through the mire of material, constantly tripping themselves up, before finding something that approximates to a meaningful insight for the patient. Because of the inevitability of errors in shorter-term work, the Therapeutic Alliance has to be strong, and so is cultivated sooner and more energetically than in psychoanalysis.

In addition, broad spectrum workers in the public sector have to deal with team policies, politics and personalities from which the private analyst is cushioned. These can adversely affect the treatment if the therapist is unable or untrained to appreciate staff dynamics or to represent and fight for her patient's rights (without alienating everybody).

And so all too often the supervisor finds herself having to supplement the training the supervisee has already undergone, if problems resulting particularly from lack of Assessment are to be prevented in future. Many difficulties brought to supervision cannot be helped much in the present because the situation so resembles an attempt to close the stable door after the horse has bolted.

(c) Problems connected with Referral and Setting

A new supervisee brings a patient who she is worried is going to leave, and wants to know how she can stop him, and what she has done wrong to bring about such an awful situation.

I ask what sequence of events led up to the wish to leave, insisting (to her ill-concealed annoyance) she start from the very beginning.

Abe, who was 19, was the only son of a religious, but not extreme, Jewish family. There had never been problems before, but Abe's father had last year been to the GP worried sick that Abe was involved with a weird Eastern cult. He begged for referral to a specialist to see if Abe was going through some psychological crisis.

The GP gave him my supervisee's home number (she was in private practice). Dad made an appointment for him and my supervisee said she would be pleased to see the patient, providing Dad accepted that their discussions would be confidential and if he wanted information about the therapy, he would have to ask Abe. Dad agreed.

Abe turned out to be emotionally flat, talking in a monotone, answering questions in the briefest way possible. If Abe was to be believed he had always obeyed his father in all things, never quarrelled with him or his mother, and had enjoyed a quiet but uneventful life till now. A university friend introduced him to the 'cult' which he attended weekly while the rest of his life went on as normal, and apart from lecture fees to the religious leader he had parted with no money. He had come to see the supervisee to humour his father, who he felt was worrying unnecessarily and who would soon settle down when he realised how innocent everything was.

The therapy, if it could be called such, paid for by Dad, dragged on for six months, the patient continuing to be polite but quite unable (or unwilling?) to show any real emotion.

Then one night Abe's father rang the supervisee at home, announcing that Abe was moving into a communal house with other devotees and that when he had demanded to know what his therapist made of this, Abe had announced also that he was leaving therapy. This was a complete surprise to my supervisee.

In the next session the supervisee told Abe about the call and he admitted with a sigh that yes he was leaving home and the therapy. His spiritual teacher advised against therapy and he must obey. Clearly he had been more involved with this religious group than he had ever let on.

The supervisee raised with him the question of who ran his life, himself or his spiritual adviser? Had he not just exchanged blind obedience to his dad for blind obedience to the religious group? He raised an eyebrow and asked quietly: 'And if I listen to you, wouldn't that be blind obedience to my therapist?'

The supervisee was shocked. 'But you came to me for help. How can I help you if you go to these people? Couldn't you put it off, decide later?'

What supervisory help does this therapist need? None with this patient, for he left immediately. But an identification of mistakes made with this case could help her with future, similar ones.

First, she took a referral from a GP without a formal referral letter or discussion as to the nature of the problem. She took his word that there was a problem and that it was one that should be helped with psychotherapy. She did not even know if the GP had ever met the patient, let alone if he was qualified to make even an initial diagnosis. It is important to get to know one's referrers!

Second, she let the patient's father make the first appointment, so had no guarantee that Abe himself wanted help: all the subsequent signs suggested he was just keeping his father happy.

Third, she made no Assessment. Was the dull and passive exterior real or did it mask a lot of hostility to father and therapist? Was Abe blindly obeying new masters who held him in thrall, or was he choosing to free himself from an oppressive father? Was the patient doing something developmentally helpful or becoming even more reclusive and emotionally remote, unable to decide anything for himself? One answer to these questions would indicate that he was doing very well thank you, and another that some help toward independence might be in order, providing he himself wanted to work at it.

This case, so like many others, shows how eager supervisees can waste everyone's time, including their own and that of the agency for whom they work, by not educating their referrers to make proper referrals, or by at least making clear to them that all patients will be given a clinical Assessment, after which the assessing therapist will report back with recommendations for future action, the taking on of the patient herself being only one among many options.

As to the setting, I am constantly amazed at how much and how often a supervisee underestimates the power of the surroundings she provides to influence the course of therapy. She often looks for the most complex reasons for a piece of behaviour or feeling in the patient, or complains that she cannot locate any transference in the welter of material at her disposal, when both of these problems can be sorted out just by noting her patient's reaction to any change in the setting (which includes the way she looks, dresses, speaks and behaves), or his reaction to any alteration in the administrative aspects of therapy – holidays, appointment times, liaison with referrer and so on.

Comments on the setting and administration are invariably comments on the transference, giving vital clues as to the patient's preoccupations; clues that especially in the early stages of treatment, an uncertain, unallied patient would be careful to avoid dropping by addressing the therapist directly.

For example, at home where I work privately part time, I recently had to get my couch re-stuffed and re-covered as despite an elegant top, the bottom was literally hanging out and I feared an embarrassing accident.

One usually reticent, newish patient spent the whole session on the new couch creatively playing with the old saying: 'He who has made his bed must lie on it.' He felt that I, not he, was making his bed and then unfairly forcing him to lie on it, just as his mother had in sending him, without any consultation, to a strict boarding school, then, despite his complaints, blaming him years later for bad exam results and surly moods that eventually resulted in expulsion. Till now he had successfully managed to avoid all discussion of his childhood.

Another patient (who had spent much of his life in India) grumpily talked about a bed of nails and a fascinating discussion followed my seizing upon this comment. We looked at his sexual confusion, his dread that if he did not impale women with his penis in intercourse, then they would in some way impale him first, as I was doing with my new couch.

A dependent and fragile patient complained that all the squashiness had gone out of it and she couldn't snuggle down any more. She implied that I cared more for the decor of my room than her comfort and security. It was the first time she had ever been able to complain and even now could only do so indirectly.

Only one patient, with whom there had been something of a breakthrough at the end of a gruelling session the previous week, rejoiced at the new couch, throwing away the cushion he usually propped under his psychogenic 'bad back', crowing: *'Now* you'll have to believe my pain was real. This hard couch (this tough therapy?) is just what I needed all along!'

Another patient who sat in a chair for her sessions was angry that the couch had been re-covered but not the chairs. Why were the couch people getting preferential treatment? This was a clear reference to her sibling rivalry problems that were at the root of her presenting complaints.

Supervisees often need help to see the obvious, but supervisors, unwilling to seem patronising, are sometimes so reluctant to comment that they conspire not to see it either.

3   ISSUES BROUGHT UP BY INTERPERSONAL PROCESS IN THE SUPERVISION

Supervisors vary enormously in how much weight they give to this phenomenon, where supervisor and supervisee become unwittingly caught up in the very problems they are trying to solve. The patient/therapist relationship and the supervisee/supervisor relationship begin to mirror each other in the supervision session and some observation and study of this can be enlightening.

Here is a straightforward example:

Tamsin was a young, recently-qualified nurse/therapist working in what I considered to be an impossible environment. Her mental health team colleagues could not support her as they were so involved in professional rivalries among themselves, while simultaneously trying to sort out divided loyalties to the team as a whole and their individual hierarchies outside the team e.g. social work, psychiatric nursing and occupational therapy.

The details of each patient she presented, referred to the team by a GP and then allocated to her at a team meeting, were always submerged by wave upon wave of anxiety in her, seemingly about the patient, but in fact about the complete lack of boundaries and support within the team. Because she had had a formal therapy training the most impossible patients were dumped on her without any real Assessment first, and she was then expected to work miracles with them in a very few sessions.

After a few weeks I found myself becoming exhausted, looking desperately but in vain for more useful things to say to her, feeling I had reached my limit as a supervisor and was not doing any good at all. I took her a few minutes over time at each session and then found I had little energy for the next patient. I thought I must be getting old, could not sustain my concentration as I used to. I even started feeling that maybe it really was time I was put out to grass.

One morning, dreading her arrival and feeling bad about this, I suddenly realised I was mirroring the way she felt with her patients, unable to help them, exhausted by trying to do the impossible yet carrying on trying to do it. She was being foolishly heroic with her patients as I was being foolishly heroic with her.

I confided my feelings to her and at first she was terribly apologetic for wearing me out. I refused to allow her to add this to her already existing pile of stress. Eventually she was able to look with me at the process between the two of us over recent weeks as an exact copy of how she felt with her patients.

She had thought the solution might be more supervision but could afford neither the time nor the money so was getting even more stressed. I was trying to help by squeezing two sessions into one, talking twice as fast and probably getting half as much work done! We both felt better, though the team problems remained, when we stopped blaming ourselves, as supervisor and therapist respectively and tried to work out how, where and when some boundaries could be put around the work she was doing, which in great part was going to involve her saying no – something both she and I were patently bad at!

The Institute of Marital Studies at the Tavistock Clinic has studied this phenomenon in some depth and incorporated it into its supervisory techniques. Interested readers are referred to Janet Mattinson's book (1992): *The Reflection Process in Casework Supervision* and to Searles's paper (1965): 'The informational value of the supervisor's emotional experience', where this process was first described.

When such a process shows itself in supervision it needs attending to, but personally I would guard against always searching for it. Very often it is simply not there and sometimes when it is but faintly there, it gets 'done to death' by eager supervisors who are fascinated by it, at the expense of more pressing needs in the supervisee.

For myself, I tend to scan the interpersonal process in supervision for mirroring when I am stuck or stumped as I was with Tamsin, above. I see it as contributing to the work of supervision by facilitating a more subjective appreciation in the supervisor of what is happening between patient and supervisee, but it rarely, if ever, offers a complete solution to a clinical problem.

The next chapter deals mainly with aiding the supervisee to

structure and conceptualise the clinical work she is doing, rather than just bringing to supervision the story of 'what happened next'; it ends with a brief commentary on teaching clinical technique.

10 CLINICAL TEACHING IN SUPERVISION (2)

4. PROBLEMS IN ORGANISING MATERIAL

The fourth group of problems presented by supervisees concerns those that result when both parties have a rough idea of what is going wrong, but cannot take the matter further because the supervisee is experiencing difficulty in organising and presenting her material. She cannot yet build her own structure, her personal model of the kind of therapy she does, placing its current version on the table between herself and her supervisor like an architect showing his model to the client, where it can be turned this way and that, inspected from above and below, to find out where the problem occurs, as well as where the model's strengths and aesthetic appeal lie (for it should never be forgotten that supervision aims to firm up the already good points in a supervisee's work, not just help her with the weak areas).

Many questions from supervisees like: 'Should I make an exception and write a letter/send a postcard from holiday/grant an extra session to/accept gifts from this patient?' can only be properly addressed by recourse to that therapist's model erected to represent that particular session of that particular therapy. General rules and regulations about such matters are useful to beginning therapists, preventing them from straying too far from the straight and narrow path; but everyone knows there are exceptions to every rule and that the best therapists are flexible (not sloppy!) therapists. It is the ability to structure the material coherently into a working – as opposed to static – model that makes it safe to be flexible; for with one glance the therapist can see whether a course of action would firm the walls of, create leaks in, make more room in, confine things more safely within, or bring toppling down her therapeutic 'building'.

All experienced therapists are architects, even if they are no longer consciously aware of their building activities. Constructing variations of their basic model has become second nature, each session of each therapy throwing up its own mini version. Because structuring is so automatic for them, many supervisors ignore the fact that their supervisee may not yet have developed any architectural style and feels very lost. She may need to borrow structures until she can build her own; may need access to a few dusty old plans from the supervisor's archives that the supervisor herself has long forgotten.

I have known several senior therapy trainers who have evolved the most elegant and elaborate metaphors for psychotherapy and who teach delighted students how to build, say, a music model of therapy, complete with tone, colour, theme, melody, counterpoint and so on; different sorts of treatment, or sections of treatment being constructed like a sonata, or great symphony. Others compare doing therapy with the painting of a picture – the patient being a canvas of various degrees of absorbency and texture, having been painted and repainted on before. I had a colleague once who was an ardent potholer and taught his trainees about therapy as a series of interconnecting underground caves full of dark, unknown mysteries and spectacular unsuspected beauty, all hidden from the world, but findable if you knew how to read and respect nature's clues.

I am afraid my own model pales before these poetic creations, but all I can say is that it works for me and I would like to share it, at least to demonstrate the importance of having a model at all. I call my model: The Balloon in the Box. It is a visual way of ordering and thinking about any therapeutic situation under study by supervisee and supervisor, be this a single treatment session, a given moment of a session, or a selected group of sessions (i.e. a particular phase of therapy).

To understand the diagrams that follow, it is imperative to bear in mind all the time the notion of therapy as a *process between two people*. Psychotherapy is not a *thing*, a set of techniques, a collection of events. Like any other process it *moves, develops, degenerates, regenerates, can adapt or die*. And like all processes it can only occur within a *structure*.

Take a simple example: the making of a cup of tea. One might say the *process* involved is 'boiling the water', just as in making a patient better the process is called 'doing therapy'. But water cannot be boiled except in a container – the kettle, which is designed to suit that particular process. Imagine a kettle with no lid: the water would evaporate. Imagine a lid but no spout: as it heated up the container would eventually explode. The kettle (structure) *accommodates* the process. In the same way, many lidless or spoutless therapies explode or evaporate while the desperate super-visee, seeing what is about to happen, fiddles uselessly with the *process*, blind to the *structure* in which it lies, and which she needs to adapt as a matter of urgency.

My Balloon in the Box model attempts to demonstrate the *structure* of psychotherapy in simplified form, and show its critical relationship to the *process* of the therapy going on inside it. I will describe each part of the *structure* in turn, discussing how it can adapt to the *process* or be adapted by it, giving some clinical examples. I will then describe a couple of instances of adaptational failure, resulting in no therapeutic 'tea'.

THE BALLOON IN THE BOX

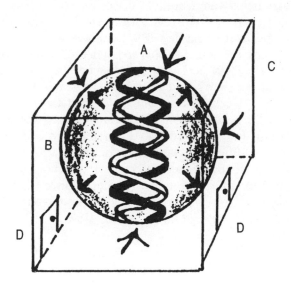

Key:
A. Transference/Alliance
   double helix.
B. Balloon.
C. Ethical Box.
D. Doors.

Figure 10.1   The Balloon in the Box

The outward-facing arrows in Figure 10.1 represent the direction of energy generated by the process of therapy. The inward-facing arrows indicate pressures on the therapy from outside. The coming case vignettes will illustrate these. The cube is a Box of ethical considera-tions (the patient's as well as the therapist's), within which sits the

clinical boundary defining the field of therapeutic action: this I call
the Balloon. There are Doors into and out of the Box (not always
needed but there 'just in case'), jointly controlled by patient and
therapist. The shading within the Balloon represents all the material
worked on in therapy, as exemplified by the Dynamic Formulation.
The double helix stands for the space in the structure that will be
occupied by two vital strands in the therapeutic process: Transference
and Alliance. I will now take the reader through each of the above.

The Double Spiral

A represents the double helix of Transference and Alliance. Broadly
speaking the Transference is the relationship the patient unconsciously projects on to the therapist or part of the therapist, which
comes from his past, while the Alliance is the here-and-now trusting relationship that has been built between two 'real' people and
which helps them survive crises in the transference, genuine dis-
agreements, or doldrums periods in the overall therapy. (For a fuller
description see Bramley 1996, chapter 4.)

In any session the Alliance and the Transference may intertwine
so much as to be indistinguishable: the therapist is working with
both at the same time, most of the time, as illustrated in the first
diagram. It can be impossible to tell if the patient's cooperativeness
stems from an idealised transference or a collaborative attachment
based on accurate perceptions of reliability, competence etc.

On another occasion though, the therapist may become aware
that the Transference is very strong and demands working on,
while the Alliance for the moment can be left in the background.
Thus what was a double spiral of equal strength in the first diagram would now look like Figure 10.2.

Figure 10.2   Figure 10.3

The supervisee may present to the supervisor a picture of the reverse situation (Figure 10.3), the heavy wiggly line (the wiggle standing for movement) now being the Alliance that needs attention. Looking at this version of the model, supervisee and supervisor can see clearly that a supportive observation rather than a Transference one is on this occasion the intervention of choice.

Sometimes the therapist needs to move her attention from Transference to Alliance and back again as the session progresses, but at all times the strands seem separate as in Figure 10.4.

Figure 10.4

Sometimes, as when a patient insists on coming early and sitting in the therapist's garden, thus 'accidentally' meeting the previous patient as he leaves, the strand of Transference manages to wriggle its way through the neck of the Balloon and into the space round it, but still, thank goodness, confined within the Box. This is classic acting out on the patient's part, but the observant therapist can, through sensitive interpretation, draw back that strand into the Balloon (clinical boundary) and reseal the Balloon's neck. I shall say more later about this essential space round the Balloon.

The Balloon

B in Figure 10.1 is the clinical boundary that I call the stretchy Balloon, made up of all the constraints and conditions (time, place, contractual agreements, the physical setting and so forth) within which the therapeutic couple will work. Its function is to contain and protect a safe, appropriately-sized clinical space, by stretching (see Figure 10.5) or in low energy times shrinking, to accommodate or conserve the work currently in hand.

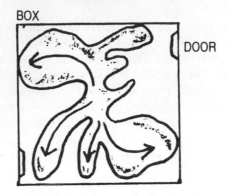

Figure 10.5   Adolescent Attempting to Act Out

Communicational energy – to be refined and converted into the process we call therapy – that is generated by the pair within the Balloon, can range from a mild pulse that keeps the Balloon stably spherical most of the time (see arrows, Figure 10.1), to a positive storm of energy. (Let's say from an angry adolescent trying his best to act out, as in Figure 10.5, but the Balloon's skin, fortified by the Box, holds him in – just!) Both these situations are examples of the elastic skin of the Balloon performing its normal and usual adaptational task.

Note that the therapist has the Doors tightly shut so that the patient, for his own protection, is kept within the Box. I shall explain both Doors and Box shortly.

The Model in a Stable State

Figure 10.1 shows a conventionally stable therapeutic situation. During Assessment patient and therapist have agreed areas on which they are going to work, and have made a Contract which clarifies all the conditions, material, administrative and psychological, within which they are to jointly labour. Figure 10.1 shows that both are honouring their obligations and duties, treating the consulting room as more or less cut off from the outside world, both physically and as symbolising a separate psychic space where mutual mental play, reflection and interpretation can occur in the absence or suspension of society's usual moral rules, codes of conduct and requirements to be at all times rational and in control.

Assuming the supervisee is seeing accurately, if each week she places on the table a model such as Figure 10.1, the supervisor can assume the therapy is proceeding without major hitch and so ethical issues are not going to arise. The Box is there, but is for the time-being redundant. Neither is the extra space within the cube but outside the Balloon going to be needed for either Balloon expansion as in Figure 10.5, or quick, competent management should the boundary – 'skin' – tear from the pressure inside it, or become too permeable, allowing clinical material to seep out. Both of these situations would leave bits of the therapy floating about within the Box and in need of urgent retrieval.

Unless something very unpredictable happens then, this (Figure 10.1) is the easiest, but not necessarily the most rewarding kind of therapy to supervise.

The Model in an Unstable (but Adaptive) State

So what might be going on inside a model presented to the supervisor that does not confirm to the basic structure of a neat spherical Balloon with plenty of space around it, safely enclosed in a stalwart Box?

Take Figure 10.5 as an example. This adolescent may very much want help but still does not trust the therapist, as a result of unreliable or conversely over-controlling authority figures earlier in his life. He is stretching the Balloon's skin as far as it will go, hurling himself at it in as many directions as possible, till it pounds against the Ethical Box and he discovers the limits to which his rebellion can go before he is finally firmly contained.

The therapist, confident of the structure she has built, so trusts the strength of her Ethical Box and the elasticity of her Balloon that she does not respond to the provocation with panic: in Assessment she had predicted just such testing of her reliability and capacity for containment. In allowing the Balloon to stretch she is permitting that necessary testing, without which the patient will never feel reassured enough to settle down; but at the same time, by holding the Box walls firm – refusing to act unethically, counter-act out – she is making them deflect his rebellious impulses back toward the Balloon's centre, where she can work on them.

For example, she tolerates then patiently explores and interprets the meaning of attacks on the Balloon – lateness, absence, rudeness, inappropriate letters and phone calls, drunkenness in the session, threats of suicide. And yet, after he has failed to show up three times and she is worried sick, she desists from breaking down the Box's walls by ringing his parents or the police, knowing that if she did she would have failed to contain the acting out and would have shown the patient he was right not to trust her.

This therapy (Figure 10.5) is holding up well in spite of difficult circumstances. The supervisee should feel encouraged.

The Dynamic Formulation – the 'Stuff' Inside the Balloon

The shading in Figure 10.1 represents the Dynamic Formulation, the 'stuff' inside the Balloon that the therapist and the patient (if at the Assessment stage he was able) have agreed needs to be worked on. The Balloon keeps all the 'stuff' in and all the unwanted, peripheral 'stuff' out.

However, on exceptional occasions the couple may elect to open the neck of the Balloon slightly to let a bit of the 'outside stuff' in, providing it is ethically proper so to do (i.e. the extra material is situated within the ethical walls making up the Box). This might happen where the original Dynamic Formulation is found to be faulty or incomplete and extra material is needed to correct it; or where unforeseen major life events – births, deaths, marriage or divorce for example, take over the patient's mental life for a time and the clinical boundary has to be opened a little to take these in. As the life crisis subsides and/or is satisfactorily dealt with, this non-priority material is allowed to seep out again, through the Balloon's permeable skin/membrane.

Permeability should be at all times under control though. Important matters like the wish for a personal relationship with the therapist are matters for dynamic understanding and interpretation *within the clinical boundary*, not matters that the Balloon should be opened up for so as to include mutual acting out in the treatment.

I knew a therapist who gave her patient a lift home every week, on the grounds that she had a polio limp and taxis were too expensive for her. The therapy failed miserably as the patient felt crushed when other favours were not forthcoming and the demand for them not analysed. The neck of the Balloon was wrongly opened the moment the therapist accepted even the possibility of giving the patient a lift rather than discussing with her what the request meant. The act of helping her into the car took the therapist way beyond the border even of the Ethical Box. There was no longer any safe space (between Balloon and Box) in which she might mend her mistake.

If the therapy is a long-term, open-ended affair, as in psychoanalysis for example, a large, floppy (gently accommodating) Balloon with plenty of 'wandering about' space is needed, any Dynamic Formulation at the early stage being quite appropriately diffuse.

There are few if any Doors in this Box, contact between the internal and external environment of the structure being unlikely as the analyst wishes to protect his vast field of study – the entire unconscious mind of the patient – from any outside 'contamination'. The start of such treatment is shown in Figure 10.6.

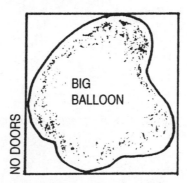

Figure 10.6 Psychoanalysis

But in short-term treatment, with a narrow, clearly-defined focus, the structure looks more like Figure 10.7. There is no 'wandering about' space for leisurely free association or for the covering of every aspect of the patient's development. There is only space for what is deemed 'top priority'.

With only once-weekly therapy and a tight time limit, the therapist must work quickly and so is more interventionist. Accordingly, the energy levels can be very high, so much room must be left within the Ethical Box for emergency Balloon expansion, even rupture. If the Balloon is too floppy, as in psychoanalysis, not only is such valuable space needlessly wasted, but lack of tautness in the 'skin' encourages wandering (in both parties!) from the Dynamic Formulation. No matter how clinically interesting such digressions and speculations are, this only results in reduction of therapeutic pressure within the Balloon and a consequent slowing of such progress as is otherwise possible within the time allowed.

The trickiest problem in short-term work is how to stick at the Formulation decided at Assessment, work on it intensively enough to produce change in the patient, but not so intensively that the pressure created ruptures the clinical boundary. The dotted line in Figure 10.7 shows where there is room for Balloon expansion, in order to prevent such a calamity. Again we are seeing structure and process successfully adapting to each other.

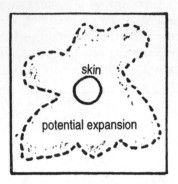

Figure 10.7   Short-term Therapy

The Ethical Box (Function 1)

The Ethical Box has two related functions. The first is to act as a safety device as in Figure 10.8. Should there be a crisis in the therapy of such proportions that the Balloon bursts – a very serious situation to be avoided if at all possible – at least there remains some space outside the Balloon but bordered by the Box, where the now homeless couple can roam while the therapist tries to mend the Balloon's skin and coax her patient back into it.

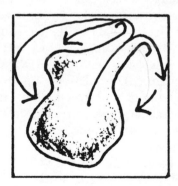

Figure 10.8   Balloon Burst, Box Walls Deflecting Escaped Energy

Very often, despite his threats, a patient in crisis after Balloon rupture does not *really* want to go home to mother / emigrate   to

Australia / return to the bottle / leave his wife and kids / kill himself; but his therapeutic home has gone and he is in panic so what else can he do? That space which lies beyond the clinical boundary but is still contained within the tough wooden Ethical Box can provide a 'halfway area' for him to wait and ponder, while repairs are carried out.

The Balloon repair will probably consist in all sorts of overt and covert negotiations to first get the patient back inside it, then a joint analysis of why the rupture occurred – this being the actual fabric of repair.

There will be letters perhaps – how much or little to put in them? Does the therapist order, invite, persuade or appeal to the Contract to get him to return? There will be the 'Who's going to ring first?' war of nerves all therapists dread; or maybe a tough line will be taken: 'Let him wait and cool down', the therapist reassured by the knowledge that he is doing his waiting in the Ethical Box space and not in the unsafe world at large.

Getting the patient back inside the clinical boundary sometimes requires meeting him half way, the therapist letting him know that *she* will attend future sessions at the appropriate time, whatever he decides, and then patiently waiting. If there were no Box for him, in which to work out his next move, such a course could be dangerous; he would already be on the plane or opening the bottle of pills.

The Ethical Box then, is a *shared* space bordered by a cube of tough wood provided by the therapist but erected by both, to protect the skin of the expandable but delicate Balloon within. In practical terms this means that when making the Contract with the patient at the conclusion of Assessment the patient is helped to see his obligations and responsibilities toward his therapist, as well as hers to him and the treatment. He now knows and believes, if contracting has gone well, that he can be as emotional as he wishes, as angry or miserable as he needs to show, but certain things are just 'not on'. Emotional demonstrations about the therapy, for instance, are for inside the Balloon, not in the world at large. Changes in the clinical boundary are matters for negotiation and/or interpretation, not psychological coercion, emotional blackmail or unilateral decision on his part. When he breaks these 'rules', which with a good Alliance become for him a shared ethos, part of his therapeutic conscience, he becomes aware, however dimly, of the Box constructed by himself and the therapist. His identification with the shared code of behaviours and attitudes of which he has agreed to be a part, makes him think twice, after

Balloon rupture, about going on to break down the walls of the shared shelter I call the Box.

It has to be recognised however, that all therapists, including the best of supervisors, have lost patients and no 'Box' is foolproof.

In summary, it can be said that the Box's first function is to facilitate reconciliation and allow space and time for emergency management after the clinical boundary has been ruptured.

The Ethical Box (Function 2)

The Box's second, equally important function, is to alert the therapist when she has behaved, or is about to behave unethically.

In addition to the Ethical Box (that stands for more than the Therapeutic Alliance but cannot be built without it) made by each patient/therapist couple, the therapist throughout her career with other patients continually develops additional, ever-thickening layers of ethical awareness that can be wrapped around it.

A mature therapist can always advise another on what, ethically, she should and should not do in a difficult case, but guiding *herself* when her emotions and perhaps counter-transference are deeply involved with a patient is quite another matter. A good supervisor, not similarly emotionally involved, can help a supervisee inspect the permanent ethical walls that do exist in her, but which for the moment she cannot see or touch. Occasionally these walls can be located during the calm of self-supervision well after the problematic session is over.

Whenever I am considering a course of action or approach with a difficult patient that I am not sure is a daring break with convention that might produce a breakthrough; or a piece of unethical conduct I have been manoeuvred into by the patient or my own vanity, I think of the Box and visualise the model. If I hear splintering I know beyond doubt I am about to do the wrong thing. This is an emergency. I heed the warning and curtail the act, even when there is no time to work out intellectually why I should not be committing the proposed action.

Gilly was a mature woman who had suffered a major breakdown and was currently functioning like a needy child. Previous therapists had given up on her because, as my referrer put it: 'She is too immature to make a treatment Alliance and seeks gratification of childish needs rather than insight. Frankly, I don't think any analytic type of work is possible.'

I had kept her in treatment for a year and she had derived much insight about her family's dynamics and the conditioning that had led to her terror of being a grown-up. But to achieve this I had had to break almost every 'rule' of dynamic therapy. She felt she would collapse when I went on holiday so I sent her postcards with encouraging messages like 'Keep your chin up till I get back'. I broke my summer holiday up into two separate periods so she would not have to be without 'mum' for too long (though I made sure she never realised this was my reason). She never manipulated me over sessions, indeed wept with a mixture of shame and gratitude whenever I went over time by a couple of minutes, or offered a kind word.

On a few occasions however, her crises were so acute and panicky I 'talked her down' on the phone, and once or twice fixed an extra session: afterwards she was always guilty, apologetic and pathetically grateful in equal measure. She was such an appealing, vulnerable and previously unloved little girl, desperate to please, I couldn't help my heart going out to her.

Therapy seemed to be progressing well, when she stepped off a bus and broke her arm and two fingers. This put paid to her recent terrified attempts to find a secretarial job, for she could no longer use the word processor. Neither could she drive, so all her friends would have to come to her. (Since the breakdown she had anyway been unable to attend any social gathering of more than three.) Her mother and father, who dismissed all her emotional problems as 'sheer neurotic nonsense' and would not discuss them, nevertheless came to her aid after the accident: physical disability they could understand – well, for a week or two.

Gilly lived only a few minutes drive or bus both from her GP and from myself. The day her visiting parents got fed up of her complaints that the broken arm made her more useless to society than ever, and walked out, she rang her GP, very upset. He made a personal call to her house after surgery and stayed for a cream tea (made by her housemate) and long chat about all manner of inconsequential things, leaving her for a while much cheered.

I knew none of this till afterwards, but the day after his visit she rang me up acutely distressed, desperately apologetic, asking if I would do a home visit on the following day when her usual session was due: she was feeling just too helpless and inferior to call a taxi; the drivers were always so nosey. She promised all in one breath that she would pay me for my travel time, that she would never do it again, that she just felt she couldn't go on without a session but that neither could she get to the session, she felt so small and weak.

I had heard her in panic before, but never so low in mood or so desperately begging in tone: she was in bad shape all right. For a split second I thought: 'Why not? She won't abuse the privilege. She never has before. It would show her that I won't walk out on her the way her parents do; it would reassure her that she mattered to me.' The accident, which wasn't her fault, had after all badly traumatised her. Her confidence, always low, was now zero. She needed support badly.

Then I heard a loud splintering in my head and without yet knowing my reasons, which could be worked out later, I said I was sorry but that it just wasn't in her interests. Let us see how she felt tomorrow after sleeping on it.

(I should point out here, that in my model the Ethical Box is invisible – unlike the clinical boundary which should be very clear indeed. Only when you bang your head against the walls of the Box do you really know where they are!)

It was myself who endured a restless night, for I felt I had let her down badly, despite knowing, deep down, that I had done the right thing. I usually discourage discussion with patients on the phone, but on a 'hunch' I had asked her, just before ringing off, if anything unusual had happened in recent days. She told me briefly about her parents' disastrous visit and how nice her GP had been about it all.

In bed I began putting two and two together and seeing what to many readers I am sure is already obvious. The stress of job hunting and socialising – of getting better in fact – was getting on top of her and the accident itself, though mightily inconvenient, solved both problems for her without having to lose face. The initial rallying round of the parents and the visit from her kindly GP was encouraging her to take up agoraphobia as yet another defence. If everyone came to her, including me, she would never have to face the world again. (However, I thought grimly, she would have to go on producing 'accidents' to justify these visits – where would that end?)

I planned my approach for the next day, both supportive and analytic (but would she come?), then dozed off. In the event she arrived on time in a taxi, accompanied by a friend who waited in the waiting room. She looked tired and drawn but proceeded to explain to me her realisation, after her hurt reaction to my refusal, of why I had done such an apparently cruel thing. Her analysis was dead on target and I congratulated her on her understanding of my motives. (I did not confess however, that the immediate cause of my 'rejection' had been the sound of splintering wood, and as with her, it had taken me some while to sort out the whys and wherefores.)

Doors in the Ethical Box

The Ethical Box has two-way Doors (D in Figure 10.1) to allow things normally kept right out of therapy (because deemed unethical) to be brought in, and things normally kept in therapy to be allowed out. Therapist and patient discuss and decide whether, when, how often and how far to open or close these Doors. This is a very controlled, adaptive situation as opposed to the ones I shall describe where uncontrolled pressure from outside smashes through the wall of the Box and invades therapy, or pressure from within the Balloon is so great it not only ruptures the Balloon but breaks down the Box walls also (see Figure 10.9) and Doors might as well not exist. This is a failure of process/structure adaptation.

Had I yielded to the pressure of my wish to give Gilly a home visit, the model for that session would have looked like Figure 10.9 – certainly not under control!

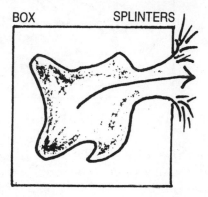

Figure 10.9 Gilly's Home visit

On one occasion Gilly's irate father phoned to ask what was happening to his daughter. She still hadn't found a job and was ringing them up for sympathy all the time, yet 18 months of treatment had gone by. I longed to try to explain to him their part in contributing to her low self-esteem, but knew that that was Gilly's right and privilege, though she wasn't yet tough enough, or willing enough to accept that they were never going to change, to do it. For the time being she still placated them.

I told them I couldn't discuss her treatment; I was sure they understood about professional confidentiality, but that there was nothing to stop them asking Gilly herself what was happening (she complained endlessly that they wouldn't talk to her). I had to do this three times before they stopped ringing me.

Had I got into dialogue with them about the therapy, not only would I have robbed Gilly of a vital part of her therapy still to come – the showdown with her parents where she did the agenda-setting for once, where she was the expert; but also I would have been colluding with them in treating her like a child unable to help herself and in need of guidance from 'us grown-ups'.

I would have failed to maintain the walls of the Ethical Box; allowed the parents to knock them down from the outside. The model would then have looked as in Figure 10.10, and I should have been heartily ashamed of myself.

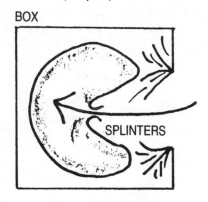

Figure 10.10 Gilly's Parents' Takeover of Therapy

I shall return to the subject of Doors in a moment, but let us for a second look at Gilly's situation some months later, when a long physical illness, an infection following a tropical holiday, kept her in hospital. What was I to do about her sessions? Certainly she could not survive emotionally without them, and she begged me to come and visit her, offering to pay my travel expenses.

The illness, as with the former arm injury, had produced enormous regression, Gilly clearly wanting me at the bedside like an attentive mum, patting the pillow and chatting affectionately about this and that. In her sessions to date I had been permitting some of this, precisely because I was protected by the Balloon and the Box. Between little bouts of playing mum I would sneak in some proper therapy, which she was willing to work on as an adult, once the emotionally ravenous little girl in her had been somewhat mollified.

A hospital visit in the usual sense would strip me of my professional setting and status and turn me into the friend/mother for which she yearned. This, though pleasant for her in the short term, would have been most unethical, for return to an ordinary therapeutic relationship afterwards would be impossible. Visiting would therefore deprive her of the continuing therapy to which she was entitled.

What I did in fact was to set up a duplicate model of our therapy. The nurses were most helpful, making available a side room, into which at a weekly specified time, Gilly walked, or if exhausted was wheeled in her bed, and there we continued our usual therapy, with a 'Do not disturb' notice on the door. No visitors, medical procedures or interruptions of any kind were allowed at this time. I never brought grapes or magazines. Fortunately I was working at a psychiatric hospital nearby and could hop over to her ward in a matter of minutes at the end of the day, so negotiation over travel expenses was unnecessary. Our replicated therapeutic structure remained unviolated.

To return to the matter of Doors (*D* in Figure 10.1) in the Box. These are entries to and exits from the structure that therapist and patient can deliberately open, or lock tightly against potentially destructive forces.

Many Student Counsellors for example, after consultation with a student who for psychological reasons is academically 'risky', will write to a tutor or examining board to furnish them with sufficient information to make a balanced judgement about staying on the course or grading an exam result. This clinical information does not escape, leak out or burst from the model; the Doors are *opened outward, deliberately and by agreement*, to let selected material through.

The Doors may be opened *inward* also.

A supervisee of mine felt she was getting nowhere with a patient who spoke very little. Yet he was able to discuss the pictures on her wall at length. Taking this up in terms of his relationship to her, she eventually realised he was trying to say that he longed to communicate with her but was a visual rather than a verbal type. She asked him if he would like to bring some images into the session that held a lot of meaning for him, whether these came from a newspaper, art gallery, advertisement, or were made by himself – any image at all.

The patient responded well to this opening of the Door by the therapist. At last he could bring in something from outside that would be of help to him inside what till now had been an alienating, because verbal, structure.

*He started by bringing landscapes that clearly mirrored his inter-
nal landscape, about which he had not before been able to speak.
Finally, before abandoning reliance on images altogether, he
brought his family photo album containing three generations' worth
of very rich material!*

Another, not so optimistic, example of Door management:

*A different supervisee, still a trainee, was attending a course that
claimed to be psychodynamic but seemed to me to enjoy barely
a nodding acquaintance with the approach. She told me she had
gone through a patient's holiday snaps with him at great length.
This, she thought, was what was meant by building an Alliance.*

*What she should have been doing was interpreting to the patient
that perhaps due to his anxiety as to what could befall him in this
unknown world of therapy, he was turning her into a harmless
'friend', which would certainly make life easier, but rob him of the
help he had come for. She missed the anxiety altogether and colluded
in a happy but useless conversation. She had opened a Door that
should have been firmly locked by a timely but non-persecuting intervention along the lines above.*

I have often been asked if photos should be allowed into a
session. A look at the Balloon in the Box and a listening out for
splintering should provide the answer, which on one occasion will
be yes, and on another, no.

THE BALLOON IN THE BOX MODEL
APPLIED TO SUPERVISION

I'd like to conclude this section on structuring the material by
applying it to the supervision session itself.

*In writing this book, one of my supervisees, who also works in a
research environment, kindly offered to help me track down certain papers and books that I needed for background reading or
for quoting in the text. I was grateful for the offer but anxious
lest time taken discussing these matters should intrude upon the
supervision session for which she was personally paying. Yet
travel and scheduling problems made it impossible for us to meet
at another time.*

We arranged a fee for her research work which was then

deducted from her supervision fee, and contracted to allocate re-
search tasks or deliver the results of them only after her supervi-
sion sessions (which preceded my lunch hour, so we had sufficient
time) were over. In this way, providing we were vigilant about it,
the supervision Balloon and Box would be preserved intact, though
the Balloon's skin would be stretched to accommodate the effect
on us both of a new research relationship which would inevitably
change our relations to some degree, although we had already
known each other for some years.

Had the research work overlapped the session, the model would
have appeared as in Figure 10.11.

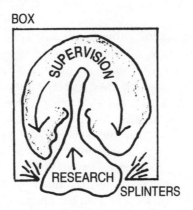

Figure 10.11   Supervision Unethically Obtruded Into

Extrusion of supervision into areas outside the Balloon in the
Box structure also represents a break with professional ethics,
though the pressure is coming from the opposite direction.

Here is an example. Colleagues often tell me of their supervisors in the NHS/voluntary sectors who, alas, also double up as
bosses and who insist on collaring them on the stairs or in the
corridor, demanding an exchange of highly confidential material
and/or a clinical opinion along with the making or amending of a
current patient's treatment package, and sometimes even wanting
to arrange a new referral! This short, rushed consultation, for
which the supervisee has had no time to prepare, is foisted on her
just as she has focussed her mind on the next psychotherapy patient she was on her way to collect when she was so unethically
interrupted. The quality of attention she can now offer that patient
is grossly diminished. That situation looks like Figure 10.12

If the matter is so urgent that it cannot wait for the scheduled

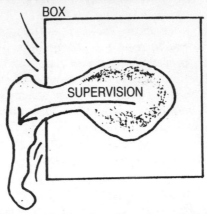

Figure 10.12   Corridor Consultation

supervision session, then a duplicate structure (in effect an emergency consultation) with all the built-in protection of Balloon and Box, should be made available. A shapeless, hastily reconstituted clinical boundary in corridor or canteen offers none of the protectors or facilitators of the proper supervision session.

In the case above, it should also be noted that there is great confusion over and overlapping between the role of clinical management and supervision. Separate structures and ideally separate personnel should be provided for each activity. If this is not possible the Balloon should have enough space in it for the two functions, which in practical terms would mean longer and more frequent supervision-cum-management sessions, such that inadequate and unethical stairway commandeering can be stopped.

Shortage of time is no excuse, especially as these rushed consultations almost always make more rather than less work for the already stressed supervisee.

5. THE TEACHING OF TECHNIQUE

I will make two simple but important observations here.

(1) Constructive use of imitation

Supervisees, especially trainees and inexperienced graduates, need concrete examples of how to phrase, time and deliver an intervention. It is rather like the medical student watching a good surgeon operate; there is no substitute for it, even in the textbook. True, the psychotherapy supervisee cannot sit in on her supervisor's treatment of a patient and watch in quite the same way, but the supervisor can nonetheless model a technique, rather than talking *about* it, by an impromptu demonstration in the supervision session, addressing the supervisee as if she were the patient being reported on. Thus the supervisee feels the impact of the technique and by identifying with her patient can tell if the supervisor has got it right.

No supervisee I have ever met has been so dim as to imitate precisely one of my demonstrations – they have all realised absolutely that they must refine what I have shown them, make it their own.

When a therapist is just starting out, abstract or theoretical advice alone can seem very limited. If she understands the meaning of what is happening with her patient, the supervisor is honour bound to help her to communicate (at the appropriate moment) that understanding; where necessary practising various ways to do so out loud in the supervision session. Such a supervisee is too early in her career to possess a fund of tried and trusted phrases, facial expressions and physical movements that have become second nature to her. She is understandably cautious about experimenting with verbal nuance, humour, body language – the enquiring eyebrow, the open-palmed invitation, the doubtfully chewed lip – in the treatment session itself. She sticks to the textbook. As a result she is in danger of delivering wooden interpretations in a wooden voice, using wooden, overly professional language. She is then left wondering why the patient seems not to hear.

(2) The advantages of group supervision for learning technique

There is no doubt at all in my mind that for learning new techniques very fast, a supervision group far outstrips individual supervision. In the course of colleagues' reporting on and discussion of their several patients, the supervisee is constantly exposed to how they actually *do* things in the therapy session; how often or rarely they intervene, how much or little they use slang, when why and how they joke or refrain from joking, how they word and deliver a delicately balanced intervention, how they confront without being aggressive, and so on.

After a working lifetime in psychiatric and therapeutic work I am still amazed at the amount of 'new tricks' I learn in such groups, whether I am a participant or the convenor.

It is true that access to the group leader, usually the most learned and experienced member of the group, is restricted, but so also is exposure to her weaknesses The sheer variety of learning experiences on offer in a group cannot be duplicated anywhere else and will almost certainly plug some of the gaps there are bound to be in individual supervision – no supervisor can be good at everything or teach every technique ever practised.

If it is technique then, that the supervisee wishes most to brush up on, group supervision has to be the supervision of choice. If it were up to me, every trainee would get a large helping of both during her course.

11 THE NOVICE AND THE EXPERT: TWO SHORT ACCOUNTS OF SUPERVISION

In this chapter I will compare two supervision sessions. One I conducted with a recently qualified therapist just starting sessions with me, the other I did with a supervisee of many years experience with whom I had been working for some three years on a weekly basis.

Nina Coltart contributes a chapter on the same topic in The Baby and the Bathwater *(1996) and has kindly allowed me to use her idea. However, at the time of writing this, her chapter has not been published, so if there are any similarities they are purely coincidental.*

BELLA

Very many moons ago, I was trained always to use patients' and supervisees' last names until and unless other forms of address were mutually negotiated, but in recent years I have bowed, somewhat uneasily, to modern convention and adopted the use of first names, on condition that it is always mutual.

Background

Bella was 47, once a teacher, then housewife and mother until her children grew up, when she returned to work as a therapist after doing a three-year course in 'psychodynamic counselling', on which she had found a place because of her long-term voluntary work, with the Samaritans among others. The course was fairly new but enjoyed a good reputation although I was not much acquainted with it myself and knew none of the staff.

Bella was still receiving psychotherapy once a week. It is always advisable for a new supervisor to check this out at the start. I never pry into details but like to know if the supervisee is satisfied that she is properly placed, and if she feels supported by the treatment: her answers will give important clues as to what strains I can expect in the supervision.

We exchanged our curricula vitae by post before our first session, which was arranged on the phone. She had simply heard my name on the professional grapevine and rung to enquire if I had supervision vacancies. I made it clear that neither of us was committed to anything until we had properly met. If we subsequently did work together I wanted real commitment. I did not want her feeling she had just drifted or been drawn by me into supervision: at the end of the day I wanted her to feel she had *chosen* her supervisor.

During our first meeting, whilst doubtless 'sussing each other out' irrespective of what was formally discussed, we each clarified how we understood supervision and the supervisory relationship. We discussed our mutual professional experiences, me keeping in the background so that she, not I, could decide what, in my own work record, needed elaboration or questions. To help put her at her ease – she seemed very nervous – I asked her about her voluntary work, where she felt it might differ from, or help with, her new career as a therapist.

Then we worked out what kind of contract was desirable, realistic and workable, given she had no patients yet, and as a divorcee no regular income until she earned it. We settled on fortnightly sessions starting when the first patient showed up. Ideally, I would have liked a session to prepare for his arrival but this would have put too much financial strain on Bella (she was still paying for therapy and owed the course fees). Had she been working in the public sector I would have encouraged her to attend such a session and negotiate for my supervision fee with her employers, supervision being an indispensable part of the job. As it was, we would increase the sessions to weekly as her case load grew.

It seemed that a local GP she knew socially was going to refer her patients, as well as her ex-supervisor on the course. She recognised that both of these avenues could produce complications but we accepted the reality of the difficulty of acquiring new patients when you don't yet have a reputation or professional network.

Finally I checked out the setting she was offering, to see if it was neutral, private, comfortable, warm enough, and what facilities there were – toilet, waiting room and such; whether she had thought out how to greet her patient; how she might open the session; how she would manage her farewell – would she escort the patient to the door or not? And was there a ten-minute gap before the next patient so they would not meet? It amazes me how often courses seem to ignore such basic but essential matters. However, in this case it all seemed very satisfactory.

The Supervision Session

Bella eagerly but anxiously presented her first patient. She had made careful notes.

She launched into Ralph's life story, taking me through birth, babyhood, school, his family, career, hobbies and so on. The details were taking up a lot of time and were so accurate, carefully arranged in developmental order that they felt neutral, almost dead; I could get no picture of what kind of person Ralph was. But I did not want to discourage Bella or make her feel she was doing it all wrong.

Eventually I said: 'I'm sorry to interrupt, but I wonder if you would show me the wood rather than all the trees. I need an overall picture, like: What is he complaining of? When did it start, and what else was happening at that time? Had similar things happened to him before? Then, when we have the general feel of the man, we can go back to all the data you have, to fill in the gaps.'

This was intended to be direct but tactful. Bella looked worried and then listed his symptoms – depression which followed heavy drinking, which followed a series of one-night stands or short affairs with 'Bimbos', which in turn were used to blunt the pain of falling into unrequited love, always with beautiful, remote and already attached women he knew he could never have. 'That's very oedipal, isn't it?' she enquired hopefully.

'Well, you have certainly noticed a *pattern* in the behaviour, and some motives – i.e. his need for consolation all the time to ward off misery which he always falls into anyway in the end. Now I feel I am beginning to get to know your patient. I can feel for him. I couldn't before, with all those facts.'

I wanted to discourage Bella from too hasty diagnoses and from seeking security in analytic language which in fact left her none the wiser with regard to the patient. Clearly she was going to need help to learn to tolerate not knowing what was going on in the session, an essential quality in every therapist. But this was our very first discussion about a patient. Bella and I, like herself and her patient, were building bridges to one another. It was too early to lecture her on what constituted proper *attention* to the patient, or to criticise her history taking. Both these things could be commented on later, when they showed up in reports of other patients, but when she was more trusting and less afraid of me.

Bella then went on to tell me about Ralph's earliest family life, again in great detail. I realised eventually that Ralph must have been trying to get it right with her the way she was trying to get it right with me, by placatingly recounting his life to her in tidy order from the very beginning. I asked her if this guess was right (trying to get her to look at his *way of relating*) and she said yes, he had been eager to please, full of information about himself. She had just listened and memorised it all, knowing she would soon be reporting to me.

Oh dear, I thought. 'Um, do you have any hunches about the Dynamic Formulation?' – then seeing her puzzled, frightened face, I added: 'You know, what the underlying conflicts might be, what it is he is trying to solve?'

'Er, no. I mean he wants to stop drinking, and er, get married – he's 35 now.'

'So', I said, summarising, 'we know what he wants, and we know what he actually does, which seems to defeat his objectives. He's trapped in a cycle of failure; no wonder he's miserable. Now, we also know a lot of facts about his childhood. But what do we know about his key *relationships*, then and now?'

'As I said, three sisters, grandparents, a mum and dad ...' She trailed off.

'OK. But can you tell or guess, after two sessions, who meant most and least to him, and why? Who was a rival, who a friend, who a disappointment, who a real delight? Where are the losses, separations, frustrations? Where the triumphs and idyllic times, if any? Where, when and with whom did he feel things went wrong? Ask yourself these sorts of questions; ask them of each period of his life, not only of early childhood ... Or ask *him* even, if he is using all the session time obsessively relating facts instead of feelings.'

Bella looked shocked. 'Ask *Ralph*?'

'Why not? You'll never get the sense of where and why he is really hurting if you don't get his emotional as well as factual story. We need to know about his attachments and their quality. Intimate or distant? Cerebral or passionate? Dependent or authoritarian? Aggressive, competitive, passive? What was their duration and their strength and what conflicts did they produce in him? Were there other compensatory or balancing relationships in his life at that time, or just reinforcing ones?'

'But that would mean interrupting. It would mean asking questions. It would mean breaking his flow ...'

'Certainly that needs guarding against once therapy proper is under way, but I assume after only two sessions you are still in the Assessment stage, still deciding if you are the most suitable therapist for him, and if so how much you'll need to adjust your technique, how long his treatment might last ...'

'Well, no-o. I mean, the doctor said he needed to talk to somebody. He's a very experienced doctor. If he thinks I should treat Ralph ...'

Bella hadn't thought Assessment was necessary, so we spent some time discussing why it was essential for every patient referred to her. At this stage in her career some were going to be just too difficult, some not suited to private practice where she worked alone and without back-up services, and some were going to benefit from a different kind of help or agency that she could put their way. She had been clinging to a touching but dangerous belief that taking on allcomers was all right as long as she had a good supervisor. I was able to make a joke about this and our chuckling together helped us establish a less formal atmosphere.

Bella thought a bit more about Assessment, while I sat quietly attentive. She started asking herself, aloud, a lot of questions which I made no attempt to answer, for it was learning to ask the right *questions* that mattered most for Bella. She began to see for herself that she had no idea what capacity for self-reflection this patient had, and therefore how helpful or otherwise dynamic work might be to him. She realised there must be varying degrees of drinking and she had no idea if he were addicted or not, whether he might need detoxifying at some point, or support from AA. Was he ever violent when drunk? Would he come to sessions drunk and what would she do if he did? Was drink the real problem anyway, or just the result of the problem?

Bella's face was etched with alarm, but I smiled at her. 'Now, *now* you are thinking like a good Assessor. There'll be lots of time later to find out if he was breast- or bottle-fed, or thrown from his pram when he was two – what we need first is an overview, so as to get the beginnings, the inklings of what is really bugging him; in what area of his mental life the primary problem lies, and whether the resources you are able to offer can meet the therapeutic need ...'

Bella was now worried and excited at the same time. She felt liberated by the idea that she could actually have a conversation with the patient, ask him to elaborate things, or gently interrupt to ask him what he *felt* about the incident or person he was describing; but at the same time she felt all this was not real psychodynamic work. It was not free association. It was not blank screen. It was not the genuine article. What she meant was that it was not the strict psychoanalytic technique she had been taught.

We then had to talk about the differences and similarities between the broad spectrum work for which she had opted and the practice of classical analysis for which she had not. She was somewhat reassured to find that after Assessment I offered the couch, took much more of a passive role, and always encouraged the patient to say whatever was on his mind. Perhaps I wasn't such a heretic after all!

Bella then wanted to know about the Dynamic Formulation. I was aware how far into the session we were and what remained to be done today, so I said that as she was due to see Ralph again before we next met, and she now had a rather different slant on how she might interact with him, why didn't we leave this matter till then, so that rather than talk *about* the Dynamic Formulation, we could actually have a shot at making Ralph's, together? Hands on stuff.

Her enthusiastic reaction to this made me feel Bella was at last 'with' me. Here was the start of the working alliance in supervision that is the equivalent of the Therapeutic Alliance in therapy. She was full of questions and ideas, no longer 'on her best behaviour'.

But her face soon clouded. 'I think I've got this Assessment idea now', she said, 'but if you don't mind my saying, it sounds a bit controlling. I mean, when does the patient get to say his bit? In the first session how can he say what's up if I am starting in a planned, structured way so as to get all the material I need? Or do I just sort of let him witter on and jump in occasionally to steer him along the more interesting paths? That means the paths I want, of course. Whose session is it anyway, his or mine?'

'Good question', I replied. 'The session is *for* him, of course; but that does not mean he is talking to a lamppost. He has come to you for help. To give it you have to *do* things and *be* things. You let him begin where he wants to and you follow him. But you have an eye to the space in front of him too, the one into which he is proposing to step. You want to keep him safe – not coddled, safe! So, till he is therapeutically-speaking a bit older, you guide and protect, encourage him to go forward, play, experiment, open up; yet you respect his fear, his defences, while all the time watching and listening, coming closer to understanding him through the relationship you are together making, a relationship which enables him to tell you what for so long he has needed to speak, as well as what you need to hear in order to make sense of that speaking. A two-way shaping process. What the text books mean by "interaction".'

'And that's not interfering? Taking away his freedom?'

'Not if it's done sensitively, respectfully. Haven't we all seen "progressive" parents who have let their kids do what they like, *neglected* them in the name of freedom – let them antagonise others unchecked, emotionally hurt themselves with no subsequent teaching or explanation; allowed them to miss out on education, proper food even; let them indulge every whim, forgo mastery of self-discipline, the learning about the differences between exploiting people and having relationships with them, and then say "I was just giving him his independence"? Kids have to be helped to know and constructively use the world, and patients have to be helped to use therapy. That means helped to communicate with their therapist, not just with themselves, their pain and their need.'

'But some parents – and therapists – do dominate, take over. Where do you draw the line?'

'Mmm. Another good question. You see, we therapists are not trying to control so much as to contain ...'

'Oh, that's Bion. I never really understood. Everybody talks about it, but, well, what does it mean exactly?'

I decided to try to answer this because containment was so relevant to the managing of this patient.

The trouble with supervising is that unlike writing, where the processor can edit and re-edit till a satisfactory definition is attained, questions have to be dealt with on the spot, and so the answers aren't always ideal. One can only do one's best at the time.

'Look', I said, talking off the top of my head, 'suppose you have something precious, vital, to give your child. Well, let's take the obvious example – milk. A mother must feed her child milk so it can grow strong and healthy. But the child must neither drown in an excess of the milk that is supposed to save him nor starve because it has all drained away before he has located it and learned first that it is food and not poison, and then how to feed himself with it. There has to be a safe, water-tight *container* – be it breast, cup, bottle, jug; so the milk is saved, can neither splash all over him nor drain away: thus the right measure can be given and taken at the right intervals. No now or never panic, plenty of time, the milk will keep.'

'So my Assessment will be a kind of jug for all Ralph's problems, calm him down. Is that it?'

'You can't cure him instantly. But you can, with your Assessment, which includes the Therapeutic Alliance and your Dynamic Formulation, make the therapeutic situation safe, *contained*. Then, in post-Assessment therapy, there is plenty of time to empty the jug, a bit at a time, examine some of the contents in detail and digest them, before putting back the rest for another "feed" (session) later.'

'Too many therapists drown or starve their frightened new patient', I went on, aware I was lecturing, and maybe drowning my supervisee, 'because they possess no Assessment "jug" in which to keep safe a carefully prepared Dynamic Formulation of his psychological situation while they help him see, approach and use the jug in his own way and time. To attempt therapy proper before Assessment is as daft and dangerous as forcing an infant, for want of a sterilised bottle, to drink straight from the cow. If he's lucky he'll thrive. If he's not, he'll be underfed, overfed, poisoned or infected. At the very least he'll be traumatised out of his wits.'

I did not want to use our time to go into a long academic discussion about containment so tried to explain it as simply as possible in relation to Assessment, which was our 'topic of the day'. Theory always goes down better, I think, when related to actual practice.

With only ten minutes to go, embarrassingly aware that I was still in lecturing mode, I raised the question of referral procedures. This was the first time in the session I myself introduced a topic; I suspected Bella had not realised its importance and so would not raise it herself. She was expecting more referrals any day; we had to address it.

Bella told me about the casual way Ralph was referred and the alleged 'confidence' she and the GP had in one another, so that no letter was needed! This led to a fruitful discussion about those therapies doomed from the start because the referral is clinically inappropriate (hence the importance of Assessment after the patient arrives), or because the patient feels dragged or blackmailed into treatment (often the clue here is that someone other than the patient makes the appointment, as Ralph's GP did), or because the referrer and therapist do not know each other well enough, or know each other too well and don't dare risk offending one another by appearing to criticise (Bella's social relationship could be a problem here).

Like many non-medical therapists, Bella felt intimidated by doctors and assumed they possessed psychological knowledge which very few in fact have. She saw the GP as hierarchically superior to her and the thought of 'educating' him about how, when and what problems to refer absolutely terrified her.

Bella had been out of the professional field for some twenty years and had not begun to realise how much the NHS in particular had changed since her day. Her own confidence was poor and her professional self-esteem worse. It was vital that I should keep this in mind when supervising her, and not bombard her with too much 'advice' too soon. It was critical too, that I should notice and comment upon each step forward she made, so that along with my unavoidable criticisms she would sense my support and goodwill.

Poor self-esteem in a therapist leading to underconfidence in handling the session is not good for the patient, who often ends up theraping the therapist, and certainly never dares to confront her. Should he suffer similar lack of self-regard, he can scarcely be expected to take heart from the example set before him in the form of his cowering therapist! Helping the supervisee toward confidence is not just a kindness, but essential for the patient's good progress.

As we said goodbye, Bella said she had already learned a tremendous amount about the principles of Assessment, but was sorry we had not got very far with Ralph. She still didn't know what was really wrong with him. I said that Rome wasn't built in a day and Dynamic Formulations don't come instantly, but I promised her that as we progressed beyond basic principles I would try to stick to the clinical material.

'Thanks', she said. 'I suppose we have to start with principles before we can get to the practice. I remember that much from teaching college.'

'Yes, I'm sure you're right, but if I wander off into storytelling and lectures you must stop me and bring me back to the job in hand.'

'Yes, I will, now that I know you don't bite.'

I felt it had been a good session on the whole, though I remained uncertain as to whether I should have stuck more with the clinical material presented and not digressed so far into the philosophical and theoretical domain. On the other hand I always find that recently trained therapists, eager to get on with practical work, have little real appreciation of how important such attitudinal underpinnings are. From the very first session they seem to want to rush at the therapy, perform technical feats, dominate the material with their intellects and all the theory they have learned. An understanding of therapeutic philosophy can help to slow them down; empty their heads a little; encourage them to watch and wait while quietly gathering together both the delicate threads of meaning emerging from the material that

will eventually suggest a transference manifestation, and the gossa-
mer filaments of mutual recognition and trust that will eventually
become the tough rope of the Alliance.

LIZ

Background

Liz, a warm and physically attractive woman of 41, had been qualified and practising some ten years and had been seeing me weekly
for supervision for three years, paid for by her employer.

Currently she worked in a community counselling clinic jointly
financed by the local authority and a charity. She had a mixed,
mainly self-referred clientele, and was expected to do mainly short-
term work – up to three months, plus a few one-year contracts. In
addition, and as a result of her own negotiating, she was permitted
two spaces for open-ended work with very difficult patients. The
patient discussed here, Mick, was one such 'long-timer', as Liz
called them.

I had been hearing about Mick from the very start of his treatment three years ago. Aged 25, he'd originally come complaining of
a compulsion to 'borrow' fast and flashy cars, and wanted to keep
out of trouble with the police in future. He was extremely jumpy
and could not keep eye contact. He saw all his problems in practical rather than emotional terms.

Mick had quite a record of petty criminal offences, from receiving stolen goods to dealing in pathetically small amounts of canna-
bis, but the majority of offences were of joyriding, always alone.
Though bright, witty and fast thinking, he had no academic qualifications and had worked as a market stallholder, second-hand car
salesman, croupier, and dealer in dodgy watches, an occupation to
which he regularly returned when broke or unemployed. Most of
his days were spent playing pool. Girlfriends sounded immature,
grasping, and the attachments were all short-lived.

Briefly, the family history was as follows. Dad was described by
Mick as 'a born loser', but till his father died Mick had kept up
the pretence that his dad was a great guy, tough and able, just let
down by a bad world too cruel to help him. When Mick was 11,
dad had come home drunk and maudlin one night and had woken
him, sat on his bed and confided all his misery and sense of
failure. Mick, tired, confused and embarrassed, had tried not to
hear, telling himself his dad would be all right again once he had

sobered up. That night dad took an overdose of Panadol and more beer, and died in his bed. Mick never forgave himself. This guilt and grief, though not conscious, were very near the surface and were the obvious focus for the first phase of treatment.

Mother seemed affectionate but slapdash to the point of neglect, Mick often wearing the same socks for a week, his mum remembering dinner money only once in a while. He never had sports gear for school as she 'never got round to it', and he was always being laughed at by the other kids for being scruffy and disorganised. He started looking after himself from an early age. He adored his mum in spite of her shortcomings, but he could not believe her seeming lack of concern after the suicide; was shocked at her enjoyment of the spending of the insurance money. He trusted no one after that and started to abscond from school, though his mother and everyone else apparently failed to notice.

At the start of the second year of therapy Mick's mum died suddenly. Rageful recognition of her neglect along with tremendous grief became the central feature of therapy.

During the last year Mick had settled down, stopped taking cars, joined a social skills evening class, and seemed much chirpier and more confident in the sessions. But he was producing no new material.

As Liz had recently had a spate of very difficult patients, including several new ones, I had not heard about Mick for some months. (I trusted her by now, to know whom to bring and when.)

The Supervision Session

'It's Mick', sighed Liz heavily. 'He won't leave but he won't work either. We're wasting time. That long-term slot of his is precious. I've a waiting list a mile long. And the blighter just sits there and *chats.*'

'You'd better bring me up to date', I said, smiling. I liked Liz. She always had a good moan, sometimes mercilessly beating her patients to get it all off her chest, then invariably settling down to solid work in which she was always scrupulously fair, totally respecting and undeniably caring of her charges.

'Last time we talked about him', she said, 'I was complaining he never took up my hints that perhaps it was time we started thinking about ending. He was after all symptom-free and cheerful, and wasn't giving me any new material. You reminded me that though he and I had done sterling work on both bereavements it wasn't always the dramatic life events that turn out to be the essence of a successful therapy. You reminded me that Mick was an orphan long before his parents passed on; that neither had been able to give him what he needed even when they were alive.'

She counted on her fingers. 'You highlighted his emotional *neediness* now, as an adult and hence his strong attachment to me; his chronic *distrust* as exemplified by his social isolation and occasional but superficial and short relationships; and his long-standing *lack of self-esteem* as illustrated by his nicking cars and his grovelling respect and nervousness toward me at the start of therapy. *That* was the triangle that still needed treatment, you said.'

She puffed out her chest, put her head on one side, imitating me: 'The grief work was but a necessary, if painful, preliminary to the *core* of therapy.'

I laughed: 'God, what a memory.'

'Oh, I do listen you know. I've been trying to do the blooming 'core work' ever since. He won't touch it. If I go anywhere near his early childhood he mutters: "Yea, you've gotta point there", and promptly changes the subject.'

'Which you comment on?'

'Natch. We've had very frank talks about this. He admits much work remains to be done, but he feels so good now he doesn't want to disturb it. But neither does he want to go. He says he's getting a lot of benefit still.'

'From his pleasure at being with you?'

'An idealised transference perhaps. But when I bring this up, he grins. "Oh I know this is a professional relationship", he says. "I can't take you to dinner or anything. Don't worry, I understand perfectly." Then he talks about the clothes he's thinking of getting, his latest "business" venture or the funny bloke he met down the pool hall.'

'I'm not sure this is transference at all', I commented, 'idealised or otherwise. He is *actually*, not in fantasy, getting good things from you, things he never had – attention, intelligent conversation, respect. You are an attractive girlfriend who wants to listen to, not exploit him, and a caring mother who'd never forget his football togs, all rolled into one. There's no "as if" you were like that. You *are* like that.'

'Come again?'

'Well, imagine his week. Not exactly full is it? No esteem-feeding work or friends, or even hobbies to occupy his thoughts. Imagine him killing time in the pool hall for hours on end, dreaming, not unrealistic dreams of fame, fast cars and the high life any longer, but perhaps of the real women – not empty-headed dolly birds – that could be his, now he is so much better. Women like you.'

Liz's jaw dropped.

'After all', I went on, 'he no longer cowers and stutters before you, does he? You told me he has abandoned the old jeans and he shaves for every session now. He reads literary books from the library and discusses them with you. He *chats*. Can't you see he is having a *real* relationship with you? He is enjoying you and enjoying himself. He is getting confidence from relating to you and it feels great.'

'Crikey, I never realised it was quite like that. I mean, well, this won't do will it? I have to help him transfer that new skill to others. Now I think of it, he's not taken a girl out for months.' She frowned, thought a bit. 'His not bringing up new material – that's not only because he is scared to revisit the distant past, which I accurately picked up; but also because he doesn't want therapy at all at this point, he wants a *relationship*.'

'Attagirl', I said.

Liz, these days, could always be counted on to take up any idea, hint or hunch proffered and work on it herself. I'd barely get a sentence out and she'd be finishing it for me, before elaborating on it. I think this was not just her own eager personality, but also the result of my having always held back to let her work things out for herself, rather than stealing her sense of achievement by insisting on giving her a finished product. She was now a very independent thinker.

'Perhaps I should allow him the relationship for a while', she mused aloud, 'as a bit of practice, a trial run for a proper one with someone else. If I keep commenting on it instead of just letting it happen I'll only make him self-conscious: he may think he is doing something wrong. But while he is practising in this way – oh goody, I don't feel he's wasting time now, I feel he is profitably *using* me! – I must take advantage of it, get him back to child-hood, how it felt being lonely, unloved, teased ...'

'Except you've tried it and he won't play.'

'Well, I'll just have to try again, won't I?'

'You can't bully or enthuse him into producing material, you know.'

'But I can't just sit there and ... and ... *agree to be his girlfriend* can I? It's not ethical. It's false encouragement.'

'Don't be so impetuous. Does it all have to be so black and white?'

'What do you mean?'

'Not only is Mick "using you usefully" – how clinical, hence safe, that sounds! – but he also has an almighty crush on you which has to be dealt with sensitively. You must neither encourage him too much, nor slap him down for adoring you.'

'Adoring?'

'Yes, adoring', I insisted. 'When it happens to them, therapists – including myself – always underestimate the extent and power of a reaction like this, part transference maybe, but also a first real experience of love based on accurate perception. Mick really *hasn't* met anyone like you before, has never been treated the way you treat him, in his whole emotionally-impoverished life. It's heady stuff for him – and a most delicate matter of understanding and management for you.'

Liz was shaking her head disbelievingly.

'So, yes you need some shared agenda as well as the weather and last night's TV, thus risking too much collusion and falsely raising hopes, or at least filling his head with unrealisable fantasies. So what are your options?'

'I could bring it all into the open, I suppose, tell him I understand and am not critical of his enjoyment of the first three-year relationship he has ever sustained with a woman. I could even compliment him on his success. Then we could look at the implications of just talking about books and TV and such – I mean helping him to see that however pleasant it is we can't just go on like this forever ... I guess I'm trying to get him to terminate again, aren't I? I'm scared of this crush of his. Makes me feel uncomfortable.'

'It's good that you recognise that. Any other options?' I mildly enquired.

'Well, I could be kind but firm; refuse to comply with his friendly overtures. I mean I could just stay silent and poker-faced like an analyst until his chat dries up. Then he'd have to face leaving or move on to proper work ... but you know, that would take us right back to where we were three years ago. He was a jellyfish, shaking in his boots, scared witless. I only got through to him by showing a bit of normal human feeling, sort of teaching him the "how" of talking, even filling the awkward gaps for him at first, to stop him running out of the room. We've always had a couple of minutes' chat to start with, to help us get going. I can't change the habit of three years without seeming very persecutory.'

'I can understand that. But are your choices really so black and white: sack him or force him down the gloomy mines of his childhood? No middle way?'

'I give up. Spill, please.'

'Well, why not find something you can both work on without you feeling guilty of collusion or him feeling he is about to confront his worst nightmares?'

'Such as?'

'Personal confidence. What he has acquired of it with you is impressive given his past, but he isn't daft. He knows it's wafer-thin. Daren't try it on anyone else, and why bother when it is all so cosy with you, providing therapy never ends. Because of this I like your idea of telling him you accept his need to practise with you, bringing things into the open without drama or fuss; but you'd need to show that you realise it is not *only* "practice"; that you appreciate his being so fond, it honours you. You are not shocked or excited. You do not have to *do* anything about it.'

'Like interpret it out of existence, you mean? Reject him?'

'Yes. Mick needs your genuine personal tribute, your acceptance of the honour he does you, as flowers need water.'

Liz was clearly interested. She indicated that I should go on, though as ever I wasn't exactly sure where I was going. Let's hope I would know when I got there!

I said something like: 'You might then be able to steer this kind of honest conversation into an agreement that you both start a fresh phase of treatment, that of helping him to look at and understand his lack of confidence, while at the same time developing more of it in the here and now, outside the consulting room as well as in. If he gets things wrong at first "out there", he has somewhere safe with you to come and talk about it.'

Liz's face lit up. 'Hey, you mean I could actually use *our* relationship, his and mine, as part of the work? His "crush" wouldn't be a secret any more? I could acknowledge that he's doing a good job of "being a man" with me and express my wanting to help him extend it? That way I'd be accepting his feelings, wouldn't I, while making clear that I am not "available", not going to abuse his attachment feelings by gratifying them?'

'Exactly.'

'And if it works out, we're bound to get to childhood eventually, to the root of why he so lacks confidence. But he'll come to it voluntarily, gradually, through what is happening in his life now, outside ... You know, Wyn, that confident, almost cocky exterior he has developed with me over three years is but the thinnest veneer; I see that now. It needs consolidation, constant linking of past influences that contributed to the poor self-esteem, with present new social experience, so that the cockiness becomes something else, something firmer – adult charm rather than childlike sauciness, perhaps ... If rewards can be seen and felt in the form of new relationships, even if we have to start with the basics – the milkman and shopkeeper – he'll be less afraid of delving into his past; there'd be some point to it then, it wouldn't any more be just a painful exercise.'

I chewed my lip. '"Delving" doesn't sound quite right, Liz. "Approaching the past slowly, sideways, like a crab", might be a better way of putting it ...'

'Oh do stop being so solemn. I know you think I always rush things, but I'll take it slowly all right. Don't you trust my unconscious? Why do you think I took him on as a long-timer in the first place? Deep down I must have known, mustn't I?'

'I stand corrected.'

We smiled at one another. It felt as if a piece of work had just been completed. We enjoyed a little restful silence, before Liz broke in.

'I remember you saying more than once that undoing trauma, getting to root causes is only half the battle. You have to heal, re-educate, re-grow up the patient as well. Make up for the formative experiences he missed. *That* is why it's important to let Mick have this "real" relationship with me, isn't it? He is *learning* – learning what most chaps learn much sooner because they have the basic confidence to have a shot at it.'

'And I must learn to stick to time, much as I would like to continue with this. We have to stop, Liz.'

'Oh sorry, I get carried away.'

'No need for apology. It is my responsibility to manage the time, not yours.'

I trust that this account shows the degree of informality, mutual spontaneity and shared thinking that comes about in a mature supervisory relationship. Something similar should occur in therapy too, the patient and therapist developing private jokes, shared metaphors and a common language that short-circuits the careful, precise but neutral language necessary at the beginning to avoid misunderstanding.

I hope it also illustrates that when a supervisee is stuck between two apparently impossible ways forward in the therapy, there is often a middle road. Mick could not, out of fear, contract to look at a desperately unhappy childhood (and anyway was preoccupied with other, much pleasanter concerns); but he could, and eventually did, contract to work on something *associated* with that awful childhood, because it very much linked in with his current desire for more self-esteem and better relations with women.

I believe the valuable lesson which Mick and I illustrated for Liz in this session was how symptom relief so often marks the start of a new and vital phase in therapy, rather than its end. The therapist has to be patient during this transition to core therapy, for the patient is often frightened to go further and naturally wishes to enjoy his hard-won freedom from symptoms.

Some patients do indeed elect to end therapy at this point, and that is their right. But the therapist needs to have a professional view which can be shared with the patient before the final decision is taken. I believe that Liz was premature in recommending termination, which she did because of the anxiety raised in her by the intensity of Mick's feelings for her.

Mick's case also shows how important it is for supervisors to remember and teach their supervisees the need for staying with a long-term patient after he has understood his symptoms, for that is far from the end of the story. Through that understanding he will have become aware of all the normal developmental processes he missed out on or got distorted. He will be terrified at the prospect of having to catch up on them at such a late stage without external support.

Reconstruction and re-education of a damaged psyche, especially with regard to self-esteem, is as much the therapist's concern as formal disentangling treatment. What is the point in thoroughly digging over a garden and throwing out the weeds if the gardener has no idea what then to put in it? The weeds will just grow again.

A chronically damaged patient needs personal confidence, interpersonal skills and some positive life experience before he can be said to be well. Acquiring such things so late in the day can be more frightening to him than the treatment process itself. The relationship with the therapist can provide the first successful foray into the here and now world of personal relating – the first safe testing-ground. This is not the time to view and interpret everything as transference. The patient needs encouragement to extrapolate from his interpersonal success with his therapist to others outside the consulting room, at a pace he can stand, before even thinking of termination.

12 ENTITLEMENTS AND OBLIGATIONS OF SUPERVISOR AND SUPERVISEE

Throughout this book, and in its very title, supervisor and supervisee have been referred to and treated as a *couple*, thereby stressing the central importance to the enterprise of a good working *relationship*. This 'team of two' consists of much more than mere courtesy between the pair, or the respect due to a senior practitioner from a junior one. Neither does it depend on liking each other or sharing outside interests and preferences. Rarely does it come ready-made, rather it needs application by both parties and time must be allowed for this, which one-off or intermittent supervision barely permits.

However, these remarks should be balanced with a caution against monitoring the relationship so intently and often that it becomes like a plant that is constantly dug up to see how the roots are faring, only to die in the process. Once established and flourishing, the relationship can be left in peace while the task of supervision goes ahead. But as with any regular relationship, there will be peaks and troughs, stability and turbulence and both parties need to be aware of these.

Despite the heading of this final chapter it cannot be said that the working alliance on either part is an entitlement or an obligation, even though it is an absolute necessity. For it cannot be commanded into existence, only striven for; not so much by exertion or study as by a mutually open attitude and psychologically honest dealings within a firmly maintained supervision frame.

If you are to be any good as a supervisor, you must remember what it was like to be supervised. (And if as a supervisee you tremble before the seniority and experience of your supervisor, it will repay you to recall the anxiety you experienced at having to meet new patients; this is suggestive of what your supervisor is feeling – however under control those feelings may be – on first meeting *you*!)

Penelope Crick's (1991) highly readable paper vividly portrays the subjective experience of the supervisee, especially with regard to the difficulty of trainees, who, for all their 'ignorant students' status are often in midlife, carrying adult responsibilities, a wealth of clinical experience and high job status.

She highlights too, a position taken up by the good supervisor that I have always believed essential; a position which, in a traditional, well-functioning family with offspring to be brought up, would be taken by the father. Too many supervisors, beguiled by their own narcissism, competitiveness or sense of omnipotence, take over. They have to put their stamp upon, or interfere in, the therapeutic work, instead of maintaining an appropriate distance while supporting the therapeutic pair. Crick says:

> The role of the supervisor here ... is to protect the mother–baby couple from intrusions and impingements, so that they are free to get to know each other properly. A 'bad' father would be one who interferes too much and prevents the establishment of a secure relationship with the object. As time goes on, it is important that his role changes – the mother and baby each need there to be a third object to relate to and with whom to identify.

In this same paper, written when the author was herself coming to the end of traineeship, we are also reminded how vital it is for the supervisor to move from identification with the supervisee-as-therapist to identification with the patient and back again, before standing back to cast her gaze upon them as a pair. Total concentration on the supervisee's reported experience can seem very judgemental, especially where a patient is acting out or being confrontational; but over-involvement by the supervisor with the patient and his reactions to his therapist can seem just as persecutory. Observations of the treatment dyad as a *system* can be particularly helpful as the supervisee is so locked inside the system she can scarcely be objective. However, system observations should not be used defensively by the supervisor, to hide her ignorance of what might be occurring in the patient for example, or to cover a reluctance to challenge the therapist/supervisor.

Let us finally review the previous chapters and list what each party is entitled to expect from the other, and what professional obligations to one another they have to meet, if ethically and clinically supervision is going to be satisfactory.

In the first chapter I looked at similarities and differences between supervision and therapy in terms of their developmental sequence. A supervisee is entitled to a proper, if informal, assessment of whether and how the proposed supervision might work, before making what is often a long and expensive commitment which will have an enormous impact on her patients. She too will be 'testing the water' but understandably her evaluations will be more subjective and coloured by all manner of personal anxieties, just as a patient's are when meeting his therapist for the first time. Ultimately the responsibility for assessing lies with the supervisor.

The supervisor is therefore obligated to make a *professional* judgement about the viability of supervision between this particular pair; the supervisee is wise to make such an evaluation too, though not actually obligated. If she is still a trainee or only recently qualified she may, like an inexperienced patient under Assessment, be quite unable to do so.

The supervisor is also obligated to draw up a clean, mutually agreed contract and to stick to it, challenging the supervisee if and when it is ignored. Though sometimes uncomfortable this acts as a good model for the supervisee in her own work with the patient. The supervisor must practise what she preaches.

The supervisee should expect to be *kept poised* rather than *held*. Her own professional and personality resources should be fostered and developed; she should not be treated like a helpless infant, encouraged to regress and become overly dependent on her supervisor.

In the second chapter I charted and discussed specific areas of help the supervisee is entitled to expect, though how much attention is paid to each and when, will depend upon the supervisee's need and level of expertise. These areas are:

(a) clinical illumination from the supervisor;

(b) development of her ethical and philosophical understanding of psychotherapy;

(c) improvement of her theoretical knowledge and the plugging of gaps in her general therapeutic education;

(d) increased self-awareness in the job ('professional development');

(e) support, which can be as challenging as it is reassuring.

The differences between real support and collusion masquerading as support were stressed.

The next chapter advised the supervisee what to look for in selecting a supervisor, and tried to assist the beginning supervisor when entering a new partnership with a supervisee. Preparation on both sides increases the likelihood of a successful outcome. The notion of matching the right supervisor to a particular supervisee is important, though as with patients and therapists, one may have to do the best one can with the resources available. Providing both parties are mature enough to labour willingly for an eventual working alliance, good marriages can often be made out of unpromising material; but it has to be said that some couples are just non-starters and should stop before they begin. The supervisor needs to be honest with both herself and the aspirant supervisee over this and never do 'let's pretend' supervision. All that leads to is 'let's pretend' therapy!

In chapters 4 and 5 I stressed the crucial nature of self-supervision for both parties. The supervisee, as she becomes able, is obligated to think over her material before presenting it, so that it is already digested a little by the time it gets to the supervision session. Her learning will not be advanced if she merely regurgitates the patient's material and waits for the supervisor to sort it out. In the same way the supervisor needs to self-supervise her sessions with her supervisee, not to rely solely on discussions with colleagues or on some belief that being so senior no monitoring is needed.

Chapter 6 profiled some common personality traits in supervisees that can hinder work with patients and which the supervisor needs to tactfully bring into the open, under her obligation to increase the supervisee's self-awareness in the job (chapter 2).

The list of traits is not all-embracing and readers or students on supervision training courses might find it a useful exercise to draw up other profiles they have met within their own experience.

For obvious reasons the teaching of philosophy and ethics is a pivotal obligation of the supervisor. I have tried to use actual examples in my experience to demonstrate how to do this in chapters 7 and 8.

I have listed ten 'dos and don'ts' to assist the supervisee-reader to organise her thoughts about how to behave ethically in her sessions, and to remind the supervisor-reader what kind of thing she ought to be teaching under this heading. These are ten guidelines, not ten commandments, and once again the list does not claim to be all-inclusive.

The items on the list are as follows:

(a) Never underestimate your importance to the patient.

(b) Do not abuse the patient with your own need for self-regard.

(c) Do respect the patient's defences.

(d) Do not seduce or be seduced.

(e) Do not use 'bad' language.

(f) Always do a proper Assessment.

(g) Do not abandon.

(h) Do not deny a patient's world view different from your own.

(i) Do honour religious and cultural differences.

(j) Do laugh (where appropriate).

These injunctions also apply to the supervisor's dealings with her supervisee!

Chapters 9 and 10 tackled the supervisor's primary obligation to provide good clinical teaching to the supervisee, whose primary obligation in turn is to prepare and organise, if possible structure into some sort of visualisable model, and then clearly present her material for study. This much the supervisor is entitled to, if she is to be enabled to work at her best for the patient's benefit.

It should be said at once that beginner supervisees cannot yet be expected to model-build and are entitled to be helped with this problem, rather than criticised for it. Chapter 10 offered an example of how a model may be taught and demonstrated, but it is only an *example*: each supervisor will have her own model to offer. Ultimately the supervisee will build her own structure of therapy and no longer need to borrow.

Chapter 9 schematised the commonest clinical teaching problems that have appeared in my own supervising practice. I have tried to come to the supervisor's aid over these by means of case examples. It should be remembered that these problems are not always easy to identify because they present at different levels of consciousness. The more hidden ones are in danger of being neglected, but there is no excuse for this. The supervisee is entitled to expect her supervisor to keep an eye out for unconscious process in their sessions.

The scheme looks like this:

COMMON CLINICAL PROBLEMS PRESENTED FOR SUPERVISION

1. Conscious, direct requests for clinical help from the supervisee:
   (a) The Dynamic Formulation
   (b) The transference
   (c) Short-term therapy

2. Problems spotted by the supervisor, the supervisee not being aware:
   (a) Imbalance of thinking/feeling/intuiting in the supervisee
   (b) Not understanding differences between psychoanalysis and broad spectrum psychotherapy
   (c) Issues to do with the setting or referral procedures

3. Issues brought up by interpersonal process within the supervision session, i.e. 'mirroring'. The supervisor *gradually* becomes aware.

4. Difficulties experienced by the supervisee in coherently structuring her material. The supervisee rarely realises this is the problem, and her supervisor often ignores it, taking it for granted that the supervisee already has an internal model of therapy. The tendency is for both to 'decide' the problem lies in the patient.

5. How to teach and learn the actual techniques of therapy. Both are very conscious of this!

Chapter 11 contrasted two supervision sessions, one with a novice and another with an expert, illustrating, I hope, all I have tried to show throughout the book about the importance of an ever-unfolding, authentic, deeply personal but always professional relationship between the supervisory pair.

In the early stages of supervision the supervisor may have to be a little more didactic. (Don't children learn to feed themselves by at first being spoonfed and then taking over?) She may need occasionally to remind the supervisee of her contractual obligations and show her how together they need to do maintenance work on their joint setting and boundaries. Her language is clear, 'proper', tactful and supportive, even when gently criticising. At this stage the supervisor is every inch a living model of what the supervisee should aspire to in her early dealings with the patient.

In a mature supervisee/supervisor relationship, as with a mature patient/therapist relationship, the couple will have developed their own shorthand, jokes, stories; their own way of teasing, challenging, criticising each other; a whole dictionary of meanings foreign to everyone else. To an outsider their behaviour may not always seem 'correct', but it has sprung from a complex, highly specialised interactional system built by the pair over months or years, which has an internal consistency – self-regulatory balancing and checking mechanisms, flexible but firm boundaries – that allow for creative interchange and experimentation with ideas that in a less established relationship would indeed be undisciplined, even anarchic.

Having summarised the book I would like to turn finally to the vexed question of accreditation/registration. No doubt supervision too is about to come under inspection in this regard and therapists will flock to 'recognised' training courses that will spring up all over the country to meet the demand. While welcoming any move to keep up standards and protect the public, I am worried about too much standardisation; too much concern about career prospects and making sure one is part of the professional 'in crowd' at the expense of the patient, who would benefit much more from his therapist's supervisor if she had been allowed to develop the art of supervision gradually, as her own expertise and knowledge as a practitioner increased, rather than in a rushed once and for all qualifying course.

My fear is of supervisors becoming clones, intimidated by registering and academic bodies, fearful of their own originality and opinions lest they are locked out by the establishment. Alas, their 'correct' style of supervision will only show which course they attended rather than reflecting their unique therapeutic qualities developed through time, clinical experience and self-scrutiny.

When I was learning to be a therapist, before the mushrooming of courses and broadening of 'schools', we trainees had to use the same small pool of analysts for our own treatment. We made a hugely enjoyable game out of guessing who was analysed by whom. We nearly always got it right, because the trainees talked, walked, dressed partially or wholly, and often used the same facial expressions as their analysts (who we knew because they had taught us or worked with us in some other setting, or whose publications were well known).

In such an intense learning setting some unconscious imitation is inevitable, but there is a difference between the modelling process and that of inadvertent indoctrination. We must be vigilant not to repeat errors of the past; too much orthodoxy, turning books into Bibles, making institutes into churches, the supervisor now and the therapist then turning away from what is quietly growing inside their imperfect but authentic Self as a result of their actual work experience. Here, *inside*, is where real learning happens: teachers and institutes can help once the practitioner has done her own work, can by inspirational means even set that work in motion; but can never, ever provide a substitute for it.

While some formal training for the supervisor may be desirable, and voluntary discussion with colleagues at a similar level of professional development will certainly help her do a better job, I would still rather see an apprentice system, rather than a once and for all qualification system in operation. I would like to see young, qualified therapists, when they feel ready, encouraged to supervise beginners, and, as they mature, each member of the couple encouraged to move on to someone more experienced.

At the start of her supervising career the therapist can take along this new work to her own supervisor, but increasingly, *in her own time and not time set by some training course or accrediting body*, she will seek and find more self-reliance, and confidence that she carries with her the necessary 'good enough' internal resources to aid herself and others without constant support. After all, is that not what we would all like for our patients?

REFERENCES

Arundel, Jean (1993) 'Supervision: Impacts, Practices and Expectations' Ph.d thesis. Faculty of Sciences, University College London.

Barkham, Michael (1989) 'Exploratory therapy in two-plus-one sessions (1) Rationale for a brief psychotherapy model' in *British Journal of Psychotherapy*, vol. 6, no. 1.

Barkham, Michael and Hobson, Robert F. (1989) 'Exploratory therapy in two-plus-one sessions (2) A single case study in *British Journal of Psychotherapy*, vol. 6, no. 1.

Bowlby, John (1953) *Child Care and the Growth of Love*, Pelican.

Bramley, Wyn (1996) *The Broad Spectrum Psychotherapist*, Free Assocation Books.

Brennan, Richard (1993) *The Alexander Technique: Natural Poise for Health*, Element.

Casement, P. (1985) *On Learning from the Patient*, Tavistock.

Collard, Jean (1995) (Unpublished dissertation) 'Some functions of metaphor in the therapeutic setting', Oxford.

Coltart, Nina (1993) 'Attention' in *Slouching Toward Bethlehem and Further Psychoanalytic Explorations*, Free Association Books.

Coltart, Nina (1996) 'And now for something completely different ...' in *The Baby and the Bathwater*, Karnac Books.

Crick, Penelope (1991) 'Good supervision: on the experience of being supervised' in *Psychoanalytic Psychotherapy*, vol. 5, no. 3, 235–45.

Dewald, Paul (1987) *Learning Process in Psychoanalytic Supervision: Complexities and Challenges*, New York, International Universities Press.

Freud, Sigmund (1976) *The Interpretation of Dreams*, Pelican, Freud Library, vol. 4. Reprinted 1991.

Gray, John (1990) *Your Guide to the Alexander Technique*, Gollancz. New edition 1994.

Hawkins, Peter and Shohet, Robin (1989) *Supervision in the Helping Professions*, OUP. Reprinted 1991.

Hinshelwood, R.D. (1994) *Clinical Klein*, Free Association Books.

Hobson, Robert F. (1985) *Forms of Feeling*, London, Tavistock.

Jacobs, Michael (1996) 'Parallel process – confirmation and critique' in *Psychodynamic Counselling* 2.1, February.

Kubie, L.S. (1991) 'The destructive potential of humour in psychotherapy' in *Americal Journal of Psychiatry*, 127, 861–6.

Langs, Robert (1994) *Doing Supervision and Being Supervised*, Karnac Books.

Lee, Ronald and Colby, Martin J. (1991) *Psychotherapy after Kohut. A textbook of Self Psychology*, Karnac Books.

Mahrer, Alvin and Gervaize, Patricia (1984) 'An integrative review of strong laughter in psychotherapy: what it is and how it works' in *Psychotherapy*, vol. 21, no. 4, 154–60.

Mann, David (1991) 'Humour in psychotherapy' in *Psychoanalytic Psychotherapy* vol. 5, no. 2, 161–70.

Mattinson, Janet (1975) *The Reflection Process in Casework Supervision*, Tavistock Institute of Marital Studies. Second edition 1992.

Searles, Harold F. (1965) 'The informational value of the supervisor's emotional experience' in *Collected Papers on Schizophrenia and Related Subjects*, The Hogarth Press and the Institute of Psychoanalysis.

Sharpe, Meg (1994) *The Third Eye: Supervision of Analytic Groups*, International Library of Group Psychotherapy and Group Process. Routledge.

Viorst, Judith (1986) *Necessary Losses*, London, Sydney, New York, Tokyo, Toronto, Simon and Schuster.

Winnicott, Donald W. (1947) 'Hate in the countertransference' in *Collected Papers: Through Paediatrics to Psychoanalysis*, London, Tavistock Publications.

Winnicott, Donald W. (1971) *Playing and Reality*, London, Tavistock.

FURTHER READING

Baker, Ronald (1993) 'Some reflections on humour in psychoanalysis' in *International Journal of Psychoanalysis* 74, 951–9.

Cade, Brian W. (1992) 'Humour and creativity' in *Journal of Family Therapy*, 4, 35–42.

Christie, George L. 'Some psychoanalytic aspects of humour' in *International Journal of Psychoanalysis*, 75, 479–89.

Haig, Robin A. 1986) 'Therapeutic uses of humour' in *American Journal of Psychotherapy*, vol. XL, no. 4, 543–53.
Langs, Robert (1978) 'A model of supervision: the patient as unconscious supervisor' in *Techniques of Transition*, New York, London, Jason Aronsen, Inc, ch. 19, 587–625.
Ryle, Anthony (1990) *Cognitive Analytic Therapy: Active Participation in Change*, Wiley.
Schon, Donald A. (1987) *Educating the Reflective Practitioner*, San Francisco, Jossey Bass.

TRAINING COURSES IN SUPERVISION

Adult Education Department, Leicester University.

Department of Continuing Education, Birmingham University.

Westminster Pastoral Foundation, 28 Kensington Square, London W8 5HN.

INDEX

Index by Judith Lavender